2-minu...

Messages

for
Communion
Celebrations

Jim Townsend

Group
Loveland, Colorado

Dedication

I thank God for my own rich heritage of communion from growing up in the Brethren Assemblies, and in particular for my mentor-in-communion, Eddie Schwartz.

Two-Minute Messages for Communion Celebrations
Copyright © 2003 Jim Townsend

Visit our Web site: **www.grouppublishing.com**

All rights reserved. No part of this book may be reproduced in any manner whatsoever without prior written permission from the publisher, except where noted in the text and in the case of brief quotations embodied in critical articles and reviews. For information, write Permissions, Group Publishing, Inc., Dept. PD, P.O. Box 481, Loveland, CO 80539.

Credits
Editor: Brad Lewis
Acquisitions Editor: Paul Woods
Chief Creative Officer: Joani Schultz
Copy Editor: Dena Twinem
Art Director/Print Production Artist: Jane Parenteau
Illustrator: Christian Musselman
Cover Art Director: Jeff Storm
Production Manager: Peggy Naylor

Unless otherwise noted, Scripture taken from the HOLY BIBLE, NEW INTERNATIONAL VERSION®. Copyright © 1973, 1978, 1984 by International Bible Society. Used by permission of Zondervan Publishing House. All rights reserved.

Library of Congress Cataloging-in-Publication Data
Townsend, Jim, 1943-
 Two-minute messages for Communion celebrations / by Jim Townsend.
    p. cm.
Includes indexes.
  ISBN 0-7644-2568-4 (pbk. : alk. paper)
  1. Lord's Supper--Sermons. 2. Lord's Supper--Meditations.
  3. Plymouth Brethren--Sermons. 4. Sermons, American. I. Title.
  BV4257.5.T69 2003
  264'.36--dc21   2003005304

10 9 8 7 6 5 4 3 2 1   12 11 10 09 08 07 06 05 04 03

Printed in the United States of America.

Contents

INTRODUCTION 4

1—REMEMBRANCE:
Meditations on the Concept of Communion 7

2—IN THE BEGINNING:
Meditations From Israel's History 21

3—POETRY AND PROPHECY:
Meditations From Psalms and the Prophets 45

4—MINISTRY OF JESUS:
Meditations From the Gospels. 61

5—SALVATION AND RIGHTEOUSNESS:
Meditations From Romans 73

6—THE EARLY CHURCH:
Meditations From the Epistles. 79

7—THE HIGH PRIEST:
Meditations From Hebrews. 103

8—UNVEILING THE FUTURE:
Meditations From Revelation. 113

SCRIPTURE INDEX. 119

STORY TITLE INDEX 125

Introduction

Whether it's at a fried-chicken-and-potato-salad picnic on the Fourth of July or turkey-with-all-the-fixings dinner on Christmas Day, most of us have a sincere and deep longing to get together with our families. Once we're in the same room, we laugh and reminisce about old times, catch up with what's going on now, and talk about the exciting times the future might hold.

For believers, communion is like a gathering of our extended families—a celebration with our family of God. We solemnly remember the sacrifice Christ made through his death on the cross. We celebrate his resurrection. We share with our community of faith and with God as we celebrate. And we excitedly look forward to the future when Jesus will return.

Jesus instituted communion (or the Lord's Supper or the Eucharist as different traditions refer to it) on the night he was betrayed when he took some bread and wine and taught a profound object lesson. He took the bread, blessed it, and broke it for his disciples. Then he took a cup of wine, blessed it, and had each of the disciples drink. In doing so, he provided symbols of his coming death, calling the bread "my body given for you" (Luke 22:19) and the wine "the new covenant in my blood" (Luke 22:20).

In 1 Corinthians 11:24-25, Paul reminds us that Jesus said, "Do this in remembrance of me." In fact, many pastors speak those words as the people in their congregations partake of the communion elements. As we carry out Christ's command concerning communion—some churches do so as often as every Sunday—we need to admit that anything we do with relentless regularity can easily become "old hat."

That's where this book comes in—to give fresh insights into the meaning of communion. The goal is for these one hundred meditations to serve as stand-alone ideas to use at a moment's notice, as well as to serve as spark plugs for your own additional ideas.

How you use this resource is up to you. Because they're so brief, you might simply decide to scan the meditations to see which one will most easily tie in to your planned sermon. Or check the Scripture index on page 119 to see if it includes a verse or passage from your teaching text.

This book also includes several special features that you may or may not feel are appropriate in your own church setting. For variety, I haven't included every feature in every meditation—in fact, some include only a main Scripture reference and the portion you should speak aloud. These features are noted throughout the text. They are:

Scripture. Every meditation includes this feature. While you'll find these and other verses noted in the Scripture index, the Scripture listed is usually the primary text that the meditation is based on, or it may be a related passage that encapsulates the focus of the message.

Background. This is background information for you. It may be guidance for a story you want to tell as you move into your communion service, a bit of background or history related to the meditation, something you'll put into your own words, or a reminiscence of mine that may spark your own thoughts.

What to Say. These words, set apart with a bold typeface, should be spoken aloud to a group or congregation. You can read them directly from this book or paraphrase them in your sermon notes or on a page tucked into your Bible.

Interactive Idea. Often, the more that people are involved and interact during teaching, the more information they'll retain and use in real life.

Use the Unusual. This is a grown-up version of "show and tell" that will also allow you to incorporate something memorable into your communion time.

Object Lesson. While word pictures are wonderful, a *visual* image can enhance the *verbal,* so I sometimes suggest using an object for its symbolic significance.

Finally, note that the label Two-Minute Messages is a bit misleading. You might stretch these ideas into much longer meditations on communion. Similarly, if you read only the "What to Say" section of some of these meditations, the message might be much shorter than two minutes!

However you plan and use these ideas, remember that communion celebrations can be one of the richest aspects of church participation—if the mood and majesty of its meaning come through in the demeanor and treatment of those leading it. As you lead, pray that the beauty of the Lord will rest upon you and shine through you for his glory.

—Jim Townsend

Chapter 1
Remembrance:
Meditations on the Concept of Communion

The "Comm" in Communion

Three P's

Precious Memories—Let Them Linger

Golden Arches

From Sign to Signified

Kuriakon

Communion Cairns

Christ's Collectibles

Great Expectations

The Invisible Inviter

Once Upon a Time, Far Away

"Otherishness" Over Selfishness

The "Comm" in Communion
Scripture: Hebrews 13:16

▼ ▼ ▼ ▼ ▼ ▼ ▼ ▼ ▼ ▼ ▼ ▼ ▼ ▼ ▼ ▼ ▼ ▼

WHAT TO SAY

As we partake of the elements of communion, I want to talk about the first four letters in the word *communion*. Notice that like *community* and *communication*, *communion* has the root *comm*. All these words express the idea of commonality or sharing.

As Christians, we get together in *community* because of our joint faith in Christ. Oddly, what we share in common is most uncommon as the world sees it. We often express the idea of community with the term "fellowship."

In some churches, the people who partake of communion together are called "communicants." Hebrews 13:16 says that we should "not forget to do good and to share with others." It probably means sharing of our substance—financially. In a similar way, when we partake of *communion*, we share spiritually.

Of course, in order to have genuine sharing, or *communion*, we must first have a true *union* with Christ by means of a new birth through faith in him. As we receive the elements today, reflect on your personal relationship with Christ, and about your unity with the community of Christ because of the common faith in Christ that you share with other Christians.

OBJECT LESSON

Even if your local congregation traditionally uses separate pieces of bread or crackers, you might wish to hold up a whole loaf of bread to illustrate the concept of unity and community. You may even choose to use a loaf rather than separate crackers.

Three P's
Scripture: 1 Corinthians 11:26

▼ ▼ ▼ ▼ ▼ ▼ ▼ ▼ ▼ ▼ ▼ ▼ ▼ ▼ ▼ ▼ ▼ ▼

USE THE UNUSUAL

Bring in a pea pod, and as you hold it up, announce, "I have three P's here—as does 1 Corinthians 11:26."

WHAT TO SAY

In 1 Corinthians 11:26 we can find three P's:

1. Participation
2. Proclamation
3. Prospect

The first line of the verse points to our participation as we "eat this bread and drink this cup." We indulge, we're involved, we interact. We participate in a joint venture and collective adventure.

Second, while we usually partake of communion indoors, Paul pronounced it a proclamation. As believers, we "proclaim the Lord's death." In other words, even the in-church experience of communion has an evangelistic element to it. As you partake of the elements today, think about how you'll proclaim the message of Christ when you leave this place.

Third, it points to our prospect. Communion is a sacrament we practice until Christ returns. Our present participation and proclamation in communion are only until Christ drinks it anew with his people in the kingdom of God, as it says in Mark 14:25.

What a memorable participation. What a meaningful proclamation. What a momentous prospect!

OBJECT LESSON

Distribute brochures or printed church invitations, and suggest that everyone give one to a friend, neighbor, or co-worker during the coming week. This will take the indoor feel of communion beyond the church doors as an outreach to your community.

Precious Memories—Let Them Linger
Scripture: Luke 22:19

▼ ▼ ▼ ▼ ▼ ▼ ▼ ▼ ▼ ▼ ▼ ▼ ▼ ▼ ▼ ▼ ▼

WHAT TO SAY

Most people—even those of us with the most sheltered of lives—have heard Barbra Streisand croon the song "Memory."

Close your eyes for a few minutes, take a few deep breaths, and think about a pleasant memory. What images come into your mind? Having the best hamburger and fries you've ever tasted in a little out-of-the-way joint? The aroma of your grandma preparing your favorite meal when you were a child? Getting lost in a sea of pages and bindings in a favorite bookstore?

At the Lord's Supper, Jesus asked us to remember him. As we celebrate communion today, engage your mind in some "precious memories" of him. Picture what it was like for him to go through the suffering he endured on the cross. Recall the emotions and warmth you felt when you first "met" him, when you began your personal relationship with him.

Remembering is not just for older people! New Testament nostalgia is for every Christian.

Christ is the central point of communion, the gravitational focus for our minds. He calls us to remember his person and work. As we share the elements of communion, ask God to bring someone to mind to whom you can lend courage by sharing a memory of your faith.

INTERACTIVE IDEA

Before you begin your time of communion, let a few people from your church tell briefly how Christ influenced and changed their lives during times of deep sorrow. Listening to these shared sorrows can enhance your congregation's appreciation of Christ's ultimate sacrifice.

Golden Arches
Scripture: Mark 4:13

▼ ▼ ▼ ▼ ▼ ▼ ▼ ▼ ▼ ▼ ▼ ▼ ▼ ▼ ▼ ▼ ▼ ▼

WHAT TO SAY

Once a woman was driving toward St. Louis. When she and her young son, Michael, came in view of the great arch above the St. Louis skyline, Michael exclaimed, "Look, Mom, McDonald's!" To many children, arches symbolize one thing only—hamburgers.

One way many Christians have viewed the physical elements involved in the Lord's Supper is by understanding them as symbols. And people relish symbols and logos. The Rock of Gibraltar symbolizes stability, solidity, security. The fox symbolizes slyness or craftiness. Jesus certainly understood the power of symbols, as he did much of his teaching through parables.

When you take the broken bread, it is something of special significance. In your ear, you might hear our loving Lord say, "This should remind you that my body was stretched on the cross for you. Remember me in my death until I come again."

And similarly, when you drink the juice [or wine], you might hear Jesus whisper, "This should remind you of my blood that I shed for you on the cross to blot out your sins. Remember me in my death until I come again."

INTERACTIVE IDEA

Before you speak, you might have individuals turn and share with one other person, or invite some to share aloud, items that symbolize something (for example, the fish symbol for Christianity, the ring for fidelity in marriage, a heart or valentine for love). You might even encourage them to take an item out of a purse or pocket to show the other person and explain its meaning. For example, a locket carried in a purse may remind the carrier of a special love relationship. Or if your worship area is equipped with a screen and projector, you might want to show photos of symbols such as these and talk about their common meanings.

From Sign to Signified
Scripture: Mark 14:22-24

▼ ▼ ▼ ▼ ▼ ▼ ▼ ▼ ▼ ▼ ▼ ▼ ▼ ▼ ▼ ▼ ▼ ▼

WHAT TO SAY

Before we take part in the Lord's Supper, I want to talk about signs. If you're old enough and you once lived in a city, you may remember using *tokens* to ride the bus. If you served in the armed services, you may have worn chevrons on the arm of your uniform as an *emblem* of your service to your country.

If you've ever traveled to Hawaii, you might have come back with fresh pineapples or cans of macadamia nuts as *mementos* of your trip. The bald eagle is a *symbol* of the United States. Our elected Congressmen and Congresswomen *represent* us in Washington, D.C.

When we partake of communion, the bread and wine serve as tokens, emblems, mementos, and symbols. We use these elements to dramatize, symbolize, represent, or signify Christ's body and blood and his death for us. These elements may be small, but they're not trivial. And while these symbols are simple, they are profound. As you eat this bread, finish this sentence silently: "For me, this piece of bread means _____." As you drink from the cup, say to yourself, "For me, the meaning of this act is _____." In that way "remember" Christ's work on the cross.

OBJECT LESSON

If you have active or former military service personnel in your congregation, ask one to bring in a uniform with sergeant stripes or some other form of military memorabilia to illustrate the significance of symbols.

Kuriakon
Scripture: 1 Corinthians 11:20

▼ ▼ ▼ ▼ ▼ ▼ ▼ ▼ ▼ ▼ ▼ ▼ ▼ ▼ ▼ ▼ ▼ ▼

WHAT TO SAY

A Greek word nestles in 1 Corinthians 11:20, and it deserves a little more attention than we usually give it. It's like an iceberg—the real significance of an iceberg is submerged beneath the surface of the ocean. I'm speaking of the term *kuriakon* [koo-REE-ah-kahn]. This word is related to the shorter Greek noun *kurios* [KOO-ree-ahss], the standard word for "Lord." While most translations render *kuriakon* as "Lord's," an adjective modifying "supper," we might render it "lordly" or "imperial" if we wanted to maximize the full force of the word.

Connecting "imperial" to the Lord's Supper might make us think of a fabulous tale, such as the story of King Arthur. This Greek word reminds us that when we celebrate communion, we are guests of His Imperial Majesty, the King of kings (Revelation 19:16). We are the knights at the round table. Or, like Mephibosheth of long ago, we are extended a royal invitation to dine regularly at His Majesty's own banquet table (2 Samuel 9:7). Imagine turning down such an invitation to such a lordly dinner!

So now, as we participate in communion, we can think of inserting ourselves into a moment of majesty. We can imagine, "I'm a guest of the King of kings. I indulge in royal food, for I am one of the King's children!"

INTERACTIVE IDEA

Ask openly if anyone has ever received an unusual invitation of any kind—perhaps to a governor's or president's inauguration. Let a few people share aloud about the circumstances of the invitation and what it involved (for example, black tie, tuxedos, evening dresses). This can naturally lead into the message that all Christians receive an imperial invitation directly from the King to take part in the remembrance of communion.

Communion Cairns
Scripture: Joshua 4:1-3

▼ ▼ ▼ ▼ ▼ ▼ ▼ ▼ ▼ ▼ ▼ ▼ ▼ ▼ ▼ ▼ ▼ ▼ ▼

OBJECT LESSON

Make some phone calls early in the week, and ask several individuals to each bring an object that serves as a memento of something meaningful in their past (such as a baseball glove from childhood or a doll owned or made by a grandparent). Let each share briefly the meaning of the memento.

WHAT TO SAY

When Joshua (whose Hebrew name was the equivalent of the Greek name for Jesus) delivered God's people, they entered their land of emancipation. As they crossed over the Jordan, they experienced a miniature version of the Red Sea all over again. God's people couldn't be touched by a surging floodtide of waters. God saved them from death.

In order to celebrate and commemorate that divine deliverance, God told them to construct a cairn—a monument of twelve stones piled up to signify their salvation (Joshua 4:2-3). In the future, the children of the delivered would ask about the meaning of that memorial (Joshua 4:6-7). As parent-teachers transmitted the truth about their salvation, they had a teachable moment about their faith. The cairn brought about communication.

Communion is the Christian's cairn. Have you ever talked about the significance of communion to your children? As we partake of these elements, ask God to remind you of truths about what Christ's sacrifice means to you.

INTERACTIVE IDEA

Like a cairn, communion is intended to call up special memories. Encourage members of your congregation to make a point of talking personally with their children or other family members this week about why communion is special and what we're doing when we enter into this experience.

Christ's Collectibles
Scripture: Luke 12:24

▼ ▼ ▼ ▼ ▼ ▼ ▼ ▼ ▼ ▼ ▼ ▼ ▼ ▼ ▼ ▼ ▼ ▼

USE THE UNUSUAL

On the Sunday before communion, you might announce a "Collectibles Sunday" the following week. All who want to participate can bring items representing their hobbies or special interests (stamps, coins, sports cards, and so on). You could have all who've brought collectibles parade across the front platform and, if time allows, say just two or three sentences about what they've collected as they hold up their items for everyone to see.

WHAT TO SAY

You could write a book—or probably many books—on the myriad items people collect. Go to any craft show or flea market and you'll find people who collect everything from cereal boxes to porcelain dolls to bird nests to baseball cards. One man even collected "fwump-fwumps"—his word for those illuminated little humps between highway lanes that go "fwump-fwump" when your car crosses over them.

What may be for one person only trash to be tossed in the garbage may prove a valued collectible to another person.

Christians are Christ's collectibles. After all, he is a savior—that is, a *saver*. He gathers us as his collectibles. We are the *saved*. To him, we have great value. When we feel valued, we in turn can communicate to others that Christ values them.

What visit, what act, what encouragement can you dispense to others this week to illustrate that Christ desires to have them as his collectibles?

As you partake of communion today, enjoy Christ as you remember that you are his valued collectibles.

Great Expectations
Scripture: Philippians 1:20

▼ ▼ ▼ ▼ ▼ ▼ ▼ ▼ ▼ ▼ ▼ ▼ ▼ ▼ ▼ ▼ ▼ ▼

USE THE UNUSUAL

If you have an avid reader or a literature teacher in your congregation, ask that person to give a brief summary of Charles Dickens' book *Great Expectations*. Ask this person to focus on what the "great expectation" in the novel is about and why Dickens selected that name for the book's title. Or search on the Internet for a summary and description of this book that you can share briefly with your congregation.

WHAT TO SAY

One new Christian came to his first communion with great expectations. Moise [MO-sheh] Rosen once told about his first Christian communion.

Because of his Jewish background, he was expecting a table spread with something akin to the fullness of a Passover Seder. As a result of this great expectation, he virtually starved himself that morning in order to be ready to partake properly. Needless to say, he was disappointed when all he got for his palate was a wafer and a cuplet (not a cutlet).

Communion may seem small-sized to us. In the physical realm, it certainly won't stave off starvation. Yet we may properly entertain *great expectations* as we meet with One more vastly awe-inspiring than any president or sports star or movie celebrity. We should take adequate time and thought before communion to appreciate the greatness of the occasion.

As you take part in the Lord's Supper, consider the great expectations that await you. Expect! Eat! Enjoy him—the One who offers us great expectations.

The Invisible Inviter
Scripture: Matthew 18:20;
Hebrews 11:27

▼ ▼ ▼ ▼ ▼ ▼ ▼ ▼ ▼ ▼ ▼ ▼ ▼ ▼ ▼ ▼ ▼ ▼ ▼

WHAT TO SAY

The eloquent Charles Spurgeon wrote:
"If now, with eyes defiled and dim,
We see the signs, but see not Him;
O may His love the scales displace,
And bid us view Him face to face!"

Matthew 18:20 indicates that where several Christians gather in Christ's name, he promises to be present among them.

While the verses leading up to Matthew 18:20 deal with disciplining an overtly sinning believer, many people believe that verse 20 applies to all genuine gatherings of Christ's local churches. When we meet, he meets with us.

When Spurgeon called upon Christians to "view [Christ] face to face," what did he mean? We can't see Christ with our physical eyes. But we can see Christ as Moses did (Hebrews 11:27)—with eyes of faith. Faith gives substance to the invisible (Hebrews 11:1), so by faith we view the one who is not visible (Hebrews 11:27). The Inviter to communion—this banquet-in-miniature—is invisible to our earthly eyes. Christ is here when we are here. He's the invisible Host who invites us, as well as the Guest whom we honor. As we participate in communion today, let's honor him by doing what he asked that we do. He calls; we come. He summons; we share. He invites; we worship him.

Once Upon a Time, Far Away
Scripture: 1 Corinthians 11:17-34;
2 Peter 2:13; Jude 12

▼ ▼ ▼ ▼ ▼ ▼ ▼ ▼ ▼ ▼ ▼ ▼ ▼ ▼ ▼ ▼ ▼ ▼

BACKGROUND

The early church probably conducted communion services in a way that would seem foreign to our modern churches. While many contemporary churches offer communion as a postscript tacked onto a sermon, the early church may have celebrated communion as part of a full meal.

INTERACTIVE IDEA

Instead of treating communion as a postscript, plan a potluck dinner after a church service, where you wrap up the meal with the traditional communion elements. Using the "What to Say" section, explain that this procedure may be similar to how "breaking of bread" occurred in the early Christian church.

WHAT TO SAY

Twice in the New Testament, we find references to an early Christian practice of a "love feast" (2 Peter 2:13; Jude 12). This wasn't intended to be some perverted occasion as the words might sound now, but rather a sacred feast of brotherly love that accompanied communion. Undoubtedly, this is what Paul referred to in the first lengthy transcript of the Lord's Supper, recorded in 1 Corinthians 11:17-34.

In other words, when everyone got off work, they broke bread together (Acts 2:46), partaking of a full-scale meal. As part of this meal, they sometimes included what we now call communion or the Lord's Supper. In 1 Corinthians 11:20-21 it's evident that a whole lot of eating was going on—not merely a bite of broken bread.

Scripture *describes* this idea without *prescribing* it. We're informed that *whenever* we eat the bread and drink the cup (1 Corinthians 11:26), we celebrate Christ's atoning accomplishments on our behalf. Just as we might have children carry palm branches on Palm Sunday to enter more fully into the spirit of the occasion, we can enter more fully into a reconstruction of early church communion by partaking in the larger framework of a full meal. So today we broaden our experience as we look at communion in a slightly different way.

"Otherishness" Over Selfishness
Scripture: 1 Corinthians 11:20-22, 33; Galatians 2:10

▼ ▼ ▼ ▼ ▼ ▼ ▼ ▼ ▼ ▼ ▼ ▼ ▼ ▼ ▼ ▼ ▼

BACKGROUND

In 1 Corinthians 11, Paul scolds Christians in the early church for participating in communion while violating the feelings of others. Having a *spiritual* experience while overlooking the obvious *social* implications to people around us turns us into phonies.

WHAT TO SAY

At perhaps the first recorded Christian communion scene after Jesus instituted the Lord's Supper, we see the haves taking advantage of the have-nots (1 Corinthians 11:20-22, 33). **Apparently, some people were starving while some of society's upper crust were gorging themselves and even getting drunk during communion!**

We don't turn communion into such a mockery—or do we? Think about it. Do we sometimes saturate ourselves in the *spiritual* significance of the bread and cup in communion, yet forget about the fact that in this biblical record of communion, Paul had to talk about its *social* significance?

The other apostles had admonished the Apostle Paul "to remember the poor" (Galatians 2:10), **which he was "eager to do." But how eager are we to remember the poor today? We can't simply remember the one who "became poor"** (2 Corinthians 8:9) **without "remember[ing] the poor"** (Galatians 2:10).

Do we have any social blind spots? God wants us to be "otherish," not selfish. What can you do this week to become more aware of the needs of poor people in our community? Remember that Jesus often comes to us in the face of the poor (Matthew 25:37-40).

INTERACTIVE IDEA

Think about the ways your local church ministers to the poor in your community. At the end of your service, take a special surprise offering for the poor. Or ask people to bring a donation of canned goods to a food pantry for the next several weeks.

Chapter 2

In the Beginning:
Meditations From Israel's History

Three Trees

From His Wounded Side

The Three Gardens

The Person of Persons

Babel and Bethlehem

Where Is the Lamb?

Isaac: Image of Christ

Jesus: Jacob's Ladder

Joseph, the Many-Paralleled

Exodus

MGM Grand Rumblings

Christ Our Tabernacle

A Tabernacle Walk-Through

Christ Our Mercy Seat

Protection From Perfection

Old Testament Object Lessons

The Scapegoat

Stadium Ramps

The Samsonesque Savior

Our Kinsman Redeemer

Covering Our Crippled Condition

What an Outdoor Barbecue

A Female Version of Jesus

Three Trees
Scripture: Genesis 2:17; 3:3

▼ ▼ ▼ ▼ ▼ ▼ ▼ ▼ ▼ ▼ ▼ ▼ ▼ ▼ ▼ ▼ ▼ ▼

USE THE UNUSUAL

If you have an artist in your congregation, ask that person to draw or paint a large poster of a tree for your use. Or pass around pieces of tree bark as you offer this meditation.

WHAT TO SAY

Today, as we approach communion, I want to talk about three trees found in Scripture, starting in the Old Testament.

The first tree sparked all of humanity's calamities. This tree grew in the garden of paradise (Genesis 2:17). When Adam and Eve tasted its forbidden fruit, their single swallow has affected our appetites ever since.

The second tree stood in the midst of other people rather than other trees. It was planted in the middle between two thieves (Matthew 27:38). Christ bore our sins in his body "on the tree" (1 Peter 2:24). How fascinating that this wooden cross was rough-hewn by some carpenter like the one who hung on it!

The first tree grew in Paradise Lost. The third tree is found in Paradise Regained (Revelation 22:2). This tree of life defies description, for it is found on each side of the celestial river. Is it like the giant redwood in California that you can drive through? This tree defies earthly explanation. But then that's eternity for you—other-worldly, description-defying, boundary-bursting, mind-boggling.

Similarly, communion engages us with something vastly beyond ourselves, for it contains dimensions of eternity. This third tree confronts us with a world greater than we've ever experienced on earth.

Praise God for these trees. By the first tree I was ruined; by the second I am reclaimed; by the third I am renovated. They encapsulate the reason we're here at communion. We recall what we were without Christ, symbolized by the first tree. We commemorate his death on the cross, symbolized by the second tree. And with the third tree, we rejoice that someday we'll enjoy eternity with him—an experience beyond all our imagination.

From His Wounded Side
Scripture: Genesis 2:21-22

▼ ▼ ▼ ▼ ▼ ▼ ▼ ▼ ▼ ▼ ▼ ▼ ▼ ▼ ▼ ▼ ▼ ▼ ▼

BACKGROUND

Adam was, in effect, given an anesthetic by the divine Surgeon. Out of that surgical sleep, God supplied him with a bride. She was taken, we might say, from his wounded side (Genesis 2:21-22). Yes, the bride to walk *by* his side was taken *from* his wounded side.

In a transcendent and mystical manner, Christ's bride (the church) might be said to be taken similarly from his wounded side.

OBJECT LESSON

If you have a large lance, sword, or very sharp-looking knife, you may wish to make use of its visual effect. A less shocking alternative is to bring in a bridal gown and hang it at the front of the auditorium.

WHAT TO SAY

Like a messianic beacon, Psalm 22:16b says, "They have pierced my hands and my feet." Remember that as Christ hung on the cross, already dead, a soldier stabbed his side with a spear (John 19:34). Out of his wound flowed "blood and water."

This "blood and water" is the true birthing of the church. The blood atones; the water cleanses. In a sense, the blood and water begat the bread and wine. We commune with Christ through the bread and cup because he sacrificed himself through the blood and water. And Paul indicates in 2 Corinthians 11:2 and Ephesians 5:25-27 that because Christians are bought with Christ's blood, we are the bride of Christ.

Today, imagine that you're experiencing your wedding day. Yes, even men can mentally pretend they are brides! What feelings and sensations run through your head as you're about to be united with your Husband? Let those sensations wash over you as you take the bread and cup.

The Three Gardens
Scripture: Genesis 2:8; Matthew 26:36; Revelation 22:1-2

▼ ▼ ▼ ▼ ▼ ▼ ▼ ▼ ▼ ▼ ▼ ▼ ▼ ▼ ▼ ▼ ▼ ▼

INTERACTIVE IDEA

As you begin this meditation, take a few moments to interview a gardener from your congregation. Do a little pre-interview planning so you and the gardener both know what to include in the interview. Ask the person to bring some gardening equipment—such as spades or seeds—to demonstrate how they're used.

WHAT TO SAY

In a real once-upon-a-time garden, humankind got under way. But our ancestors botched it badly. So they were banished from that paradise (Genesis 3:23), and so were we. Many centuries later, the second Adam (Christ) prayed desperately in the Garden of Gethsemane (Matthew 26:36). His striving—in effect—led to our thriving.

You might say that gardens are the bookends of the Bible, for the Bible begins (Genesis 2) and ends (Revelation 22:1-2) in a garden. The Heavenly Horticulturalist has been growing his fruit (John 15:1-8; Galatians 5:22-23; Philippians 1:11) in a myriad of his people-plants throughout human history. He plants, he prunes, he perfects.

Communion is one of the Great Gardener's means of stimulating our growth. He waters his ground plot (1 Corinthians 3:6-9). We accept his sun and rain, his bread and cup. We remember the one who suffered in the garden because we planted thorns in the original garden.

As you leave today, think about how you can turn your thorn into a rose this week. Perhaps your rose will be manifested in a kindly spoken word to a stranger or a batch of freshly baked cookies for a shut-in. Yes, these may mean a sacrifice. But *sacrifice* is precisely what we're remembering.

OBJECT LESSON

If you have access to thorns from roses or another thorny bush, pass a thorn to the individual communion participants after they partake of the elements.

The Person of Persons
Scripture: Luke 24:27

▼ ▼ ▼ ▼ ▼ ▼ ▼ ▼ ▼ ▼ ▼ ▼ ▼ ▼ ▼ ▼ ▼ ▼

INTERACTIVE IDEA

Ask your congregation to describe, in no more than three sentences, a character from the Old Testament who reminds them of some feature of the Lord Jesus.

WHAT TO SAY

As we approach our communion time today and recall the work of Christ on the cross, I want to look at some characters from the Old Testament. Interestingly, we see certain parallels of Christ through the very character of these individuals.

- Christ is the representative of humanity, and from his wounded side came his bride, the church. He is our Adam (1 Corinthians 15:45).
- Christ is the one through whom we find salvation from God's judgment in the ark. He is our Noah (1 Peter 3:20).
- Christ is our king of peace and righteousness who offers us bread and wine. He is our ever-living Melchizedek (Genesis 14:18; Hebrews 7:1-3). Melchizedek's name meant "king of righteousness" and his place of rulership made him "king of peace."
- Christ is the true Israel who wrestles with his obstinate people to break their stubbornness (Genesis 32:24, 28). He is our Jacob.
- Christ is the favored Son, rejected by his own family, yet providentially designed as the Savior of his world. He is our Joseph (Genesis 37–47).
- Christ is the pinnacle of prophets who was willing to endure his people's punishment (Genesis 32:30-32; Deuteronomy 18:17-20; John 6:14). He is our Moses.
- Christ is the one who led his people into God's rest. His name means "the Lord saves." He is our Joshua (Hebrews 4:8-10).

All that the Old Testament forecasted, Jesus fulfilled. All that the Old Testament concealed, he revealed. He is the sum and substance of Scripture (Luke 24:25-26) and the accent of our adoration. Oh, come, let us adore him—Christ the Lord!

Babel and Bethlehem
Scripture: Genesis 11:1-9

▼ ▼ ▼ ▼ ▼ ▼ ▼ ▼ ▼ ▼ ▼ ▼ ▼ ▼ ▼ ▼ ▼

WHAT TO SAY

Before we take part in communion today, I want to talk about two B places in Scripture—Babel and Bethlehem. *Babel* means "gate to god." When we read about the people in Genesis 11, we learn that they were building a ziggurat [ZIGG-uh-raht], or temple tower, to reach up to the heavens. This ziggurat looked like an architectural layer cake. Upward they ascended, thinking they could dethrone God or, at the very least, rule as his equal.

Babel was an early *arrogant* attempt by humankind to defy God. While we may not feel as arrogant as the people who built the tower in Babel, in our "upward mobility" we may simply be saying, "God, we don't need you." But that's sin. Sin is simply leaving God out of our lives. The other B, Bethlehem, represents God's willingness to *humble* himself (Philippians 2:8) and become man. At Bethlehem God again reinvades our lives with his wonder. Oddly, because of the impoverished context, Bethlehem is the last place we'd expect to meet God.

Similarly, we meet God in the simple context of communion. There's nothing splendid about the location or the elements. In fact, they're very simple. Yet God reaches out to us in the bread and cup.

Where Is the Lamb?
Scripture: Genesis 22:14

▼ ▼ ▼ ▼ ▼ ▼ ▼ ▼ ▼ ▼ ▼ ▼ ▼ ▼ ▼ ▼ ▼ ▼

USE THE UNUSUAL

If some children in your church have well-behaved pets or animals that are contained (such as a guinea pig in its habitat), ask these children to bring them and talk about what they like most about their pets. Ask your listeners to imagine the feelings Jewish children might have had if a pet lamb were sacrificed.

WHAT TO SAY

The Bible relates the story of an old man and a younger man trudging their way up Mount Moriah. The boy carried a stack of wood. The older of the two carried a knife blade and the fire. As the two make their way up the mountainside, the puzzled junior asks, "The fire and wood are here...but where is the lamb for the burnt offering?" (Genesis 22:7).

Ah, the lamb! This question is as natural as if we are headed to Disneyland and a child asks, "But where are the tickets?" Or, as a family has gathered for Thanksgiving and someone inquires, "But where is the turkey?"

Yes, where was the missing lamb? In emboldened, exclamatory faith Abraham announced, "God himself will provide the lamb" (Genesis 22:8). And God did.

About two thousand years later, we hear the definitive answer to Isaac's question when John the Baptist exclaims, "Look, the Lamb of God, who takes away the sin of the world!" (John 1:29).

Abraham's sacrificial lamb reminds readers of the Lamb "chosen before the creation of the world" (1 Peter 1:19-20). As we partake of the bread and cup today, picture the Lamb of God sacrificed for your sins.

Isaac: Image of Christ
Scripture: Genesis 22:7

▼ ▼ ▼ ▼ ▼ ▼ ▼ ▼ ▼ ▼ ▼ ▼ ▽ ▼ ▼ ▽ ▼ ▽ ▼

OBJECT LESSON

Carry an armful of firewood or pile it on your church's platform to represent Isaac carrying firewood up Mount Moriah.

WHAT TO SAY

See Isaac. And through him see Christ.

The writer of Hebrews refers to Isaac as Abraham's "one and only son" (11:17) even though Abraham also physically fathered Ishmael. John calls Christ God's "one and only Son" (John 3:16).

Isaac plodded up Mount Moriah at his father's instigation even as God the Son did everything that pleased God the Father. In fact, Bible scholars believe that Mount Moriah was in the very vicinity of Mount Calvary.

Isaac seems to have been the silent type. At least he uttered no words of protest (other than the innocent question in Genesis 22:7). Similarly, the Lord Jesus "made no threats" (1 Peter 2:23).

Isaac carried the very wood he was to be sacrificed on even as Jesus carried the wood of his cross. Isaac was the child of promise who God's people filtered their hopes through; Jesus was the focus of promise that the strands of humanity's hope were tied to.

God spared Isaac from his tragic and sacrificial inferno. And that's where this comparison ends: God "did not spare his own Son, but gave him up for us all" (Romans 8:32).

In communion we meditate upon the supreme sacrifice of the Son of God, the beloved Son who was brutally—yet voluntarily—offered up for our sins. Isaac received a substitute, and we have our substitute in God's sinless Son.

As you take each of the elements today, spend a few moments silently adoring the one who walked up the mountain of suffering for you. Let your heart kneel in reverence before him.

Jesus: Jacob's Ladder
Scripture: Genesis 28:10-17

▼ ▼ ▼ ▼ ▼ ▼ ▼ ▼ ▼ ▼ ▼ ▼ ▼ ▼ ▼ ▼ ▼ ▼

BACKGROUND

Sometimes, religious people who don't understand Christ's sacrifice on the cross are exasperated in their efforts to do enough good works to merit God's favor. However, only because Christ supplied the merit for us *gratis* can we return to him our *gratitude*.

WHAT TO SAY

Nathanael was captured in a *Candid Camera* shot of sorts! When Jesus complimented him for being an authentic Israelite, Nathanael pretty much reacted like someone caught red-handed by retorting, "Howdjuh know me?!" (see John 1:47-48). Only someone with a false humility could have retorted, "Oh, I'm not really that genuine."

Not only was Nathanael the ideal Israelite (John 1:47), he was even in the ideal spot for an Israelite—under a fig tree. Old Testament verses such as 1 Kings 4:25 and Micah 4:4 depict the ideal spiritual environment for Israelites as sitting under a fig tree.

It's possible that in this sublime spot, Nathanael may have been reading Genesis 28:10-17 about the man renamed Israel who saw angels ascending and descending upon the ladder to God. This could explain why Christ staggered Nathanael by announcing, "You shall see heaven open, and the angels of God ascending and descending [not upon some stairway, but] on [me] the Son of Man." In effect, Jesus implicitly declared: I'm the ladder to God. I'm the stairway to heaven.

Through Christ's body and blood, we have our ladder to heaven. This ladder is let down from above. It stands in contrast to religiosity—our effort to build our own stairway to the skies on the building blocks of our own good works.

As you eat the bread and drink of the cup, think of the words of the old hymn "Rock of Ages":

"Nothing in my hand I bring,
Simply to Thy cross I cling."

Joseph, the Many-Paralleled Scripture: Genesis 37:3-10

▼ ▼ ▼ ▼ ▼ ▼ ▼ ▼ ▼ ▼ ▼ ▼ ▼ ▼ ▼ ▼ ▼ ▼

INTERACTIVE IDEA

Ask members of your congregation to turn to someone seated next to or in front of them and say, "I think I am like [name an animal, object, or Bible character]." Once all have had a chance to share in pairs, transition to making the following comparisons between Joseph and Jesus.

WHAT TO SAY

Many Old Testament characters foretold—through their lives—Jesus' earthly ministry. One of those individuals was Joseph.

Joseph was his father's much-loved son (Genesis 37:3). **So also, Jesus was the beloved Son of his Father** (Matthew 3:17; 17:5).

Joseph was persecuted by his own brothers (Genesis 37:4). **Like Joseph, Jesus came to his own brothers, "but his own did not receive him"** (John 1:11). **In fact, some of his own people were the instigators in his death.**

Joseph was sold as a slave (Acts 7:9). **Jesus was sold out, and he became the ultimate Servant** (Isaiah 42:1; Isaiah 53:7-8; John 13:4-5; Acts 8:30-35; and Philippians 2:7).

Joseph became, in effect, the savior of his world (Genesis 42:6). **Even though his brothers sold him into slavery, he became the only means by which they could obtain physical salvation. In Jesus, we find the one who "really is the Savior of the world"** (John 4:42).

Joseph's own brothers ended up bowing before him (Genesis 42:6). **Someday, at Jesus' name, every knee will bow to him** (Philippians 2:10).

Jesus is our divine Joseph. As we partake of these reminders of his condescension and exaltation, do we bow to him now in submission and salvation?

As we close, think about fresh ways you might show your *submission* to Christ this coming week. Perhaps as you sacrifice for someone who is hungry, or as you step out of your comfort zone in another way, you'll demonstrate your submission to the one who submitted to the cross for you.

Exodus
Scripture: Exodus 12:31-39

▼ ▼ ▼ ▼ ▼ ▼ ▼ ▼ ▼ ▼ ▼ ▼ ▼ ▼ ▼ ▼ ▼ ▼

WHAT TO SAY

The exodus was the definitive and dramatic act of God's redemption of his people in the Old Testament. The components of the word *exodus* are ex, meaning "out of," and [h]odos [HAW-dahss], meaning the "way" or "road." The Israelites took the "way out" that God miraculously provided.

In New Testament vocabulary, Jesus is "the way" to heaven (Greek: *hodos*), according to John 14:6. When Jesus was transfigured, he spoke with the key person from Old Testament law, Moses, and the principal person from Old Testament prophecy, Elijah, about his exodus. Literally, *exodus* is the Greek term for "departure."

Like the ancient Jews, we Christians have enjoyed our exodus, for we've crossed the frontier out of death into eternal life (1 John 3:14). Just as Jews celebrate their exodus in the Passover, we celebrate our exodus in communion. Thank God for showing us the way out!

As you take part in the communion service today, examine your heart. Do you need to find a way out of some addiction, some "sin that so easily entangles" you (Hebrews 12:1)? If so, I invite you to come to the front at the completion of communion for after-service prayer and counsel. Let today be a day of exodus for you.

INTERACTIVE IDEA

Ask worshippers to silently pray a simple one-line prayer: "Thank you, Lord, for the way out of [fill in the blank]." After a few moments of silence, close your service with the words "Thank you, Lord, for our exodus fulfilled through our Passover lamb, Jesus. In his name we give thanks. Amen."

MGM Grand Rumblings
Scripture: Exodus 19:18-19;
Matthew 27:51-52

▼ ▼ ▼ ▼ ▼ ▼ ▼ ▼ ▼ ▼ ▼ ▼ ▼ ▼ ▼ ▼ ▼ ▼

USE THE UNUSUAL

Move from the regular part of your service into this communion meditation by playing a brief, grandiose piece of orchestral music or famous crescendo over your auditorium's sound system.

WHAT TO SAY

MGM stands for Metro-Goldwyn-Mayer. This early film studio was known for using special effects to make a big splash.

Sometimes God gets our attention in even more momentous ways. For example, when the national constitution of Israel was adopted at Mount Sinai, the smoke-enshrouded summit of Sinai erupted with titanic trembling and thunderous rumbling (see Exodus 19:18-19).

Then consider the dramatic scripting at Mount Calvary. The stage props included

1. the torn Temple curtain (Matthew 27:51),
2. the trembling earth (Matthew 27:51),
3. the torn rocks (Matthew 27:51), and
4. the open tombs (Matthew 27:52).

Yes, Mount Sinai (the giving of the law) and Mount Calvary (the giving of the Lord) certainly proceeded with MGM-style rumblings.

In contrast with these stupendous sounds, as we approach communion, we wait in silence as soft as that described in 1 Kings 19:12 or Revelation 8:1. Silent moments inspire significant reflections as we meditate upon what Christ accomplished for us in his atonement at Calvary. A masterful orchestra crescendo can result in voluminous and beautiful noise. And a breathtaking announcement can result in stunned silence. Both are effective.

As you eat the bread and drink of the cup, allow yourself to quietly absorb the drama of Calvary in your adoration of Christ.

USE THE UNUSUAL

Have members of the congregation illustrate the sound effects of the future by reading aloud Revelation 6:12-14; 10:3-4; and 19:1, 6.

Christ Our Tabernacle
Scripture: Exodus 26

▼ ▼ ▼ ▼ ▼ ▼ ▼ ▼ ▼ ▼ ▼ ▼ ▼ ▼ ▼ ▼ ▼ ▼

OBJECT LESSON

Display a toy model of some kind: a toy sports car, a model airplane, or a ship in a bottle, for example. Talk about the intricacy and complexity of the model and the effort it would have taken for an old-fashioned wood carver or sculptor to create the model.

WHAT TO SAY

Imagine the cumbersome organizational operation involved in taking down the Old Testament Tabernacle and reassembling it all over again on a new site. On a much grander scale, it would be a little like putting together a gargantuan jigsaw puzzle on your family's coffee table—only to take it apart and reassemble it later.

The Tabernacle was the portable tent worship-center that God gave to his Old Testament people. It was tailor-made according to divine blueprint (Hebrews 8:5). Through its design, it silently shouted to the people, "You— a sinful people—can approach a holy God only through the blood of sacrifice" (see Leviticus 17:11; Hebrews 9:22).

John 1:14 informs us that Christ dwelt (more literally, *tabernacled*) among us. He is the dynamic and living equivalent of that Old Testament erector set, the Tabernacle, and what it was designed to convey.

Most of us, reading of the elaborate layout of the Old Testament Tabernacle, would be prone to ask, "Why make this so tedious, so difficult?" Perhaps God was simply conveying the need to follow his instructions to perfection.

Of course, only Christ can provide perfection for our imperfection. In Christ, God meets us. Remember during our communion time that when we meet with God, Christ is our Tabernacle. We may approach God because Christ shed his precious blood (1 Peter 1:18-19). We approach a perfect Father through his perfect Son and Savior.

A Tabernacle Walk-Through
Scripture: Exodus 25–40

▼ ▼ ▼ ▼ ▼ ▼ ▼ ▼ ▼ ▼ ▼ ▼ ▼ ▼ ▼ ▼ ▼ ▼

USE THE UNUSUAL

With a straightedge and marker, draw a picture of a maze or labyrinth on an audience-sized piece of poster board or overhead transparency. Use this drawing to make the point that sometimes we must follow a precisely prescribed plan if we want to end up at our designated destination.

WHAT TO SAY

Imagine the following conversation comparing the difference between the elaborate cleansing procedure the ancient Israelites followed and the cleansing that Christ provides.

Person 1: I have sinned. How can I be put right again? I proceed to the door of the Tabernacle.

Person 2: Christ is my door. There is no entrance apart from him. (See John 10:7; John 14:6; Acts 4:12.)

Person 1: I place my hand upon my lamb's head as I watch it die for the sin I've committed. That lamb is my substitute.

Person 2: Behold the Lamb of God offered for the world's sins. (See John 1:29.)

Person 1: A gorgeously robed priest has my interests on his heart. He intercedes for me and instructs me. His job is to take care of my need for sacrifice.

Person 2: Christ has my interests at heart and is uniquely tailored to meet my need. (See Exodus 28:6-21; Romans 8:34.)

Person 1: I can barely see the large, water-filled laver in the Tabernacle's outer court. There's plenty of water there. It looks like a bit of ocean transported into the desert.

Person 2: Christ is my cleansing. (See Hebrews 1:3; 1 John 1:7.)

Person 1: The elaborately clothed priest proceeds past the various curtains of the Tabernacle where I cannot go. (See Hebrews 9:25.)

Person 2: My High Priest passes through the curtains of the heavens where he presents himself as my atoning sacrifice. (See Romans 3:25a; Hebrews 4:14.)

Indeed, as we approach communion today, remember that Christ is our door, our substitute, our priest, and our cleansing. As you remember him through these elements, absorb that sobering and joyful reality.

Christ Our Mercy Seat
Scripture: Exodus 25:17; Romans 3:25

▼ ▼ ▼ ▼ ▼ ▼ ▼ ▼ ▼ ▼ ▼ ▼ ▼ ▼ ▼ ▼ ▼ ▼

OBJECT LESSON

To introduce this meditation, show several types of covers. For example, the cover of a sewing box prevents all the items from spilling out. A book cover or dust jacket protects the book's binding. A blanket covers a bed.

BACKGROUND

Different types of covers are used for different reasons. In the heart of Israel's worship was an "atonement cover" (Exodus 25:17).

WHAT TO SAY

In Israel's Tabernacle described in Exodus 25, there was—in effect—an empty throne seat. Later it was called the mercy seat (or more accurately, the place of propitiation [pro-pish-ee-A-shun]). Propitiation refers to the averting or turning away of God's anger.

This seat was empty because, unlike their neighbor nations, Israel worshipped an invisible God. You might say that he was the unseen occupant of that kingly seat. It was on this place of propitiation that Jewish priests made the sacrifice of atonement.

In the New Testament, Paul describes Christ as the dynamic equivalent of the Old Testament mercy seat. Romans 3:25 indicates that Christ is our place of propitiation or sacrifice of atonement.

Like the seat in Israel's Tabernacle, God's mercy seat—the cross—is also empty. The cross is empty and the tomb is empty because Christ did what no one else has ever done. He conquered death. That's why a believer's funeral is actually a cause for celebration. Because Christ lives, we shall live also—forever.

Remember his past sacrifice; rejoice in the future splendor. Through communion we worship the One who is our superlative sacrifice, our propitiation, our mercy seat.

Protection From Perfection
Scripture: Habakkuk 1:13

▼ ▼ ▼ ▼ ▼ ▼ ▼ ▼ ▼ ▼ ▼ ▼ ▼ ▼ ▼ ▼ ▼

BACKGROUND

Atop the real ark of the covenant was the gold-lidded mercy seat or place of propitiation (meaning that the sacrifice was seen as covering the sins), the first piece of furniture to be described in the layout of the Old Testament Tabernacle (Exodus 25:10-22). Christ is the New Testament equivalent of the Old Testament article of furniture (Romans 3:25). He takes care of our sin problem by his supreme sacrifice.

USE THE UNUSUAL

You can probably find illustrations of the ark of the covenant in Bible encyclopedias, dictionaries, or other resource books. Ask an artist from the congregation to draw an enlarged version of an illustration of the ark of the covenant overshadowed by cherubim. Or draw an overhead layout of the Tabernacle showing where the ark was located within the Tabernacle.

WHAT TO SAY

It can be hard for us to picture the Tabernacle where ancient Israel worshipped. Imagine, though, above the Tabernacle, the glory-cloud of God's centralized *perfection*. And within the ark were two tablets of broken law, symbolizing our *imperfection*.

If nothing stood in between our imperfection and God's perfection, we might well be electrocuted by God's pure goodness. God is "too pure to look on evil" (Habakkuk 1:13). Yet the invisible shield, so to speak, between unholy people and a holy God was the mercy seat. And when Christ overcame death, he took the place of standing between heaven and humanity as the perfect invisible shield for our sin and guilt.

Christ is our mercy seat, our go-between, our interposed sacrifice, our all-atoning approach to God. "Thanks be to God for his indescribable gift" (2 Corinthians 9:15). When we take the bread and cup, it's one way we say thank you to God for all he has done.

Old Testament Object Lessons
Scripture: Matthew 22:37

▼ ▼ ▼ ▼ ▼ ▼ ▼ ▼ ▼ ▼ ▼ ▼ ▼ ▼ ▼ ▼ ▼ ▼

OBJECT LESSON

Display a jigsaw-puzzle box. If you know someone "crafty," ask that person to use special puzzle glue (available in most craft stores) to hold together a puzzle permanently, and hold that up for display as well.

WHAT TO SAY

When you're working on a jigsaw puzzle, you probably keep the top of the box nearby for reference. Similarly, the Old Testament provides a picture of the coming Christ. He is

- **the slaughtered clothing for the first sinners** (Genesis 3:21). **No one but God made a sacrifice for Adam and Eve's sin.**
- **the ark of security sparing us from God's judgment** (Genesis 6:14; 1 Peter 3:20), **even as Noah was delivered from judgment upon his world.**
- **the one who sends his servant to fetch a bride for his son** (Genesis 24:1-4; Ephesians 5:25-27), **just as Abraham delegated a servant to find Isaac's bride.**
- **the perfect Passover lamb** (1 Corinthians 5:7).
- **our guiding pillar of protection by night and day** (Exodus 13:21-22), **even as God provided a glorious, moving cloud for Israel's guidance.**
- **our supply of manna** (Exodus 16:4; John 6:32-35).
- **our tabernacle of approach to God** (Exodus 25–40; John 1:14), **for Jews approached God properly through their tent of worship.**
- **the scapegoat who not only bears our sins but shows by being sent away that our sins are gone** (Leviticus 16:10). **This was God's object lesson (a goat strutted off into no man's land), showing that all sins had been dismissed.**
- **our brass serpent of salvation** (Numbers 21:8-9; John 3:14-15), **for as those people simply looked in faith at the brass serpent, their lives were not forfeited in death.**

These are only nine of the Old Testament hints at the many-faceted work of our Savior. This shows us that our Lord Jesus is not simply one-dimensional. He invades our lives and wants to control all aspects of our lives (Matthew 22:37—heart, soul, mind). **Consider these object lessons in the coming week as you reflect on today's communion experience.**

The Scapegoat
Scripture: Leviticus 16:10, 20-22

▼ ▼ ▼ ▼ ▼ ▼ ▼ ▼ ▼ ▼ ▼ ▼ ▼ ▼ ▼ ▼ ▼ ▼

INTERACTIVE IDEA

Set aside just a few minutes for people in the congregation to turn to one other person and discuss what the word *scapegoat* means and where it might have come from.

WHAT TO SAY

Have you ever heard the word *scapegoat*? We usually use this term to describe someone who bears the blame for something someone else did. But this word came into our vocabulary straight from the Old Testament. God instituted the scapegoat in conjunction with Yom Kippur [kih-POOR]—the Day of Atonement—described in Leviticus 16.

On that momentous occasion, there was a two-goat ceremony; both goats were significant. One goat died; the other lived. One goat gave up its life; the other goat gave others life symbolically.

The scapegoat was the goat that symbolically removed the sins and guilt of the people as it was sent off into the wilderness. Imagine that goat being smacked on its flank. It looks back at the priest momentarily as if to ask, "Can I really take off?" The goat is free. It begins to trot, then picks up speed, and finally disappears. Each Israelite might exclaim, "Look! My sin and guilt are gone!"

When Christ died on the cross, he became our scapegoat so that we might escape the penalty our sins deserved. Just as the Old Testament goat symbolically carried the people's sins far away, Christ in his death has in reality carried all our sins away! Our sins are gone because he died for them and he's dismissed them. He bound himself to a cross so that we might be sin-free (Romans 6:7).

Our tokens of freedom are the bread and cup. They remind each of us "Your sins are gone. You have a scapegoat. Now you're free."

Stadium Ramps
Scripture: Deuteronomy 6:4-5

▼ ▼ ▼ ▼ ▼ ▼ ▼ ▼ ▼ ▼ ▼ ▼ ▼ ▼ ▼ ▼ ▼ ▼

WHAT TO SAY

Shema [sh-MAH] is the Hebrew word for "hear" in the command "Hear, O Israel: The Lord our God, the Lord is one" (Deuteronomy 6:4). In fact, Jewish people call this command the "Great Shema." The very next verse contains a classic command that is at the very heart of all God's people are called to do: "Love the Lord your God with all your heart and with all your soul and with all your strength" (Deuteronomy 6:5).

This command mandates three avenues of approach—heart, soul, and strength—for loving the Lord. Rather than thinking of different roads that lead to different destinations, these avenues are more like the spokes of a wheel. Or we can picture them as varying ramps proceeding into the same stadium. Though they approach the venue from different angles, they zero in on the same central object.

How do we love the Lord?

Perhaps you've been given a loving temperament. Someone sitting near you today may have more of a creative ability (such as violin playing or painting) that he or she uses to love the Lord. Another person might express his or her love of the Lord through a unique hobby. We may use these many avenues to love the Lord with all our heart, soul, and strength.

God also provides us with some significant observable objects that we can use to show our love: the Bible, baptism, and the elements of communion. And just as a small child says "I love you" with a homemade card that parents proudly tape to the refrigerator, so God accepts the love that we express by taking the bread and cup. They're our childlike way of communicating to God that we love him because God first loved us.

The Samsonesque Savior
Scripture: Judges 14–16

▼ ▼ ▼ ▼ ▼ ▼ ▼ ▼ ▼ ▼ ▼ ▼ ▼ ▼ ▼ ▼ ▼ ▼

BACKGROUND

Most people who know the story of Samson picture him as a long-haired Arnold Schwarzenegger—Mr. Muscle Man. But that may not have been the case at all. Otherwise, why would his supernatural strength have evaporated when he got a surprise haircut (which you can read about in Judges 16:17-19)?

WHAT TO SAY

Remember the story of Samson? Along with Adam and Noah, Samson is probably one of the Old Testament's best-known individuals.

Here's something you might not know about Samson—he had something of a miracle birth (Judges 13:2-3). Several characters in Scripture were born under unique circumstances: Isaac, Jacob, Samuel, John the Baptist, and, of course, Jesus, who was conceived by a virgin without a physical father. However, because of all of Samson's playboy antics, we rarely think of him as having any similarities to our Savior.

In the end, Samson possessed a combination of weakness and strength. His final tragic act meant the death of many enemies. On the other hand, Jesus' death upon a Roman crucifixion-stake seemed an act of utter weakness. Yet the Apostle Paul indicated that this "weakness of God is stronger than man's strength" (1 Corinthians 1:25).

Communion sometimes seems like a small thing, even feeble or weak. Just some bread and wine. However, through Christ's work on the cross, we receive an infusion of spiritual strength. Some of our Christian predecessors have sensed that strength so much that they even became martyrs for the faith.

As you partake of communion today, focus on the invisible infusion of strength you receive from God. With Paul, you can say those paradoxical words: "When I am weak, then I am strong" (2 Corinthians 12:10).

INTERACTIVE IDEA

You might invite several in the congregation to share times they sensed that God turned a moment of weakness in their lives into a moment of triumph.

Our Kinsman Redeemer
Scripture: Ruth 3

▼ ▼ ▼ ▼ ▼ ▼ ▼ ▼ ▼ ▼ ▼ ▼ ▼ ▼ ▼ ▼ ▼ ▼

USE THE UNUSUAL

Ask one or two married couples to tell how they met and were romantically drawn to each other. Make some phone calls well ahead of your service to come up with the most interesting stories.

WHAT TO SAY

In the lovely little book of Ruth, Boaz steps into the role of kinsman-redeemer. A kinsman-redeemer was a close relative who took over significant roles of the head of a family after that person died.

First, the kinsman-redeemer had the *power to protect.* As the owner of a big plantation, Boaz provided protection for his bride-to-be (Ruth 2:9).

In a greater way, our kinsman-redeemer, Christ, shelters us under his wings. He provides protection from eternal punishment.

Second, the kinsman-redeemer had the proper *placement of position.* He was a blood relative or relation as well as a redeemer (Ruth 3:12-13).

Christ had to become human in order to help us humans (Hebrews 2:14-17; 5:1). He was one of us—part of the fraternity of humanity. As both God and man, he was uniquely positioned in the universe to solve our problem of sin.

Third, the kinsman-redeemer had to be both *able* and *available.* He had to be *ready to relate and redeem.*

In the same way, our Messianic kinsman-redeemer declared, "Here I am...I have come to do your will, O God" (Hebrews 10:7). Therefore, he sought us and bought us.

Finally, out of Boaz as kinsman-redeemer came many children (Ruth 4:18-22).

Jesus—though a bachelor on earth—has many children (his "offspring" in Isaiah 53:10). As the family of God, we, his children, meet to elevate our household head and unparalleled kinsman-redeemer.

Christ has the capacity and the credentials to do what we can't do for ourselves. He was willing to step into our situation and serve as our redeemer.

Today, is he your redeemer? As you take the bread and cup, thank him for redeeming you.

Covering Our Crippled Condition
Scripture: 2 Samuel 4 and 9

▼ ▼ ▼ ▼ ▼ ▼ ▼ ▼ ▼ ▼ ▼ ▼ ▼ ▼ ▼ ▼ ▼ ▼

USE THE UNUSUAL

If you have any amateur or professional interior decorators in your congregation, ask them to provide special decor for your services this week. You're going for a "royal" feel, so ask them to design your platform with items such as purple wall hangings or draperies, tapestries, and any other creative furnishings that will help people think "royalty!"

WHAT TO SAY

I want to talk for a minute about Mephibosheth [meh-FIB-oh-sheth]. There's a name you have to take a running leap at to pronounce! He was a grandson of Saul, first king of the united kingdom of Israel. When he was five, his nurse dropped him, leaving him crippled for life. In those days it was risky to the neck to be a former king's grandson—it could be deadly, in fact.

Let's look at several parallels between this grandson of a king and Christians, who are children of the King of kings.

First, Mephibosheth had royal blood flowing in his veins. Need we remind ourselves that at communion we are children of the King seated at the royal table?

Second, like Mephibosheth we've been damaged by a fall. But we've been recalled to a royal position (2 Samuel 4:4; 9:6-7).

Third, all our impediments have been covered; our wounds are fully hidden beneath the covering of the King's table (2 Samuel 9:3, 7).

Like ancient Mephibosheth, we come to share the royal repast. We are enfeebled, embarrassed, and disabled by our sinful condition, yet our King graciously adopts us into his family and friendship.

Today, accept the bread and the cup as a rich remembrance of how your King cares for you.

What an Outdoor Barbecue
Scripture: 1 Kings 8:63

▼ ▼ ▼ ▼ ▼ ▼ ▼ ▼ ▼ ▼ ▼ ▼ ▼ ▼ ▼ ▼ ▼ ▼

USE THE UNUSUAL

It would be ideal if you could use this communion meditation during mild weather when you actually have scheduled a cookout after the communion. That way the church windows could be open and the aroma of grilling meat could enliven the olfactory senses of the congregation as it takes in this meditation.

WHAT TO SAY

On nearly any warm summer afternoon, you can detect that aroma in the air. Barbecue! Meat cooking outdoors over an open grill—a treat for the nose as well as for the mouth.

Imagine what Passover season in Jerusalem of long ago was like. It probably smelled like one big barbecue-feast. The sacrificial sheep are cooking on God's outdoor "stove." God even specified how the roasted lamb should be eaten (Exodus 12:8-9).

At the dedication of the Temple, King Solomon sacrificed 142,000 animals (1 Kings 8:63). What a barbecue! (Can it be found in *Ripley's Believe It or Not!*?)

Yet all those thousands of sacrifices couldn't come close to the superlative worth of the sacrifice of sacrifices, the Lamb of God. The Passover and dedication sacrifices were temporary; the Lamb's was permanent. The Old Testament sacrifices were involuntary; Christ's was voluntary. The sacrifices of lambs covered sins; Christ's sacrifice erased them for all eternity.

Relish his worth. Savor his "pricelessness." Experience his value. Bask in his majesty. Own his transcendence. Imbibe his perfume. Ingest his goodness.

Remember him.

A Female Version of Jesus
Scripture: Esther 9:19

▼ ▼ ▼ ▼ ▼ ▼ ▼ ▼ ▼ ▼ ▼ ▼ ▼ ▼ ▼ ▼ ▼ ▼ ▼

BACKGROUND

Few people think of Esther as a type of Jesus, simply because Esther was a woman. Women don't get much press in Scripture, and when they do, they normally appear in secondary roles. Esther is a rare exception, for she was married to a man who ruled more land than any other person had in history up to that point in time. But she didn't simply accept a cushy role. Her bravery exceeded her beauty. In a life-and-death matter, Esther took action.

WHAT TO SAY

Let's consider the story of Esther. In a nutshell, she was—unknown to her king—a Jewess. A man named Haman plotted to kill all the Jews. But Esther spoke up and saved the day for all the Jews in her husband's kingdom.

Esther was somewhat like Moses. Moses delivered his people; so did Esther. Esther had national power; so did Moses. Esther was a Jew facing a foreign emperor; so was Moses. Esther had a holiday named for Jewish deliverance: Purim (Esther 9:18-22); so did Moses: Passover (Exodus 12:21-30).

Just as Jews commemorate "saving" events in Passover and Purim, so Christians celebrate Christ's work on the cross in communion. Purim could be described as similar to our modern Christmas, for it's "a day for giving presents to each other" (Esther 9:19). The Last Passover merged into the first Lord's Supper (Luke 22:1, 7, 15-22; 1 Corinthians 5:7).

Esther was also somewhat like Jesus; at least she was another Old Testament character who pointed to Jesus. Esther risked her life; Jesus laid down his life. Jews remember Esther as queen of the world; Christians remember Jesus as king of the universe.

We were in a life-threatening crisis—an eternal life-threatening crisis—and Jesus put his life on the line for us. As you take the bread and the cup, ponder how you'll respond to his courageous compassion at the cross.

Chapter 3

Poetry and Prophecy:
Meditations From Psalms and the Prophets

Zoo Story

Banqueting

Beauty in the Eye of the Beholder

The Multi-Titled Messiah

Behind God's Back

Who Was That Masked Man?

Duncan Renaldo and Our Lord

He for Me

Old Testament Salvation

Where the Grapes of Wrath Are Stored

Splendor and Shame

A Whale of a Time!

Blessed by a Translation Error?

Zechariah's Pen-Portrait

Zoo Story
Scripture: Psalm 22

▼ ▼ ▼ ▼ ▼ ▼ ▼ ▼ ▼ ▼ ▼ ▼ ▼ ▼ ▼ ▼ ▼ ▼

BACKGROUND

Playwright Edward Albee authored a play titled *The Zoo Story.* While it is set near a zoo full of animals, it's the two people in the play who end up acting animalistic; one person is actually killed with a knife.

USE THE UNUSUAL

Obtain and play a tape or CD with the sounds of wild animals (such as a lion roaring, hyenas howling, and so on).

WHAT TO SAY

Psalm 22, one of the clearest classics about the coming Messiah, is in a sense our Lord's "zoo story." It foretells his crucifixion with a menagerie of attacking animals.

At the scene of the cross, encircling bulls seek to gore him (Psalm 22:12). Lions viciously rip at his flesh (Psalm 22:13). Wild dogs menace his life (Psalm 22:16). He feels like "a worm and not a man" (Psalm 22:6).

In the security of the cocoon of communion, we commemorate the savagery heaped upon Christ. While we walk in the light (1 John 1:7), we remember his nightmare of horror during the three hours of darkness. All for us. All for us.

Psalm 22 describes the anguish we deserve for our atrocities against heaven. But Heaven's Best absorbs them for us. This should elicit just one reasonable response from us—appreciation and adoration.

As you receive the bread and the cup, allow these two reminders to evoke appreciation and adoration of the One who bore our sins.

Banqueting
Scripture: Psalm 23:5;
Song of Songs 2:4

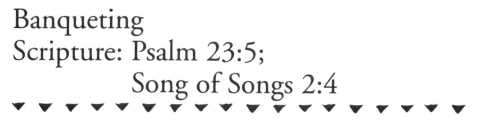

BACKGROUND

First-class hospitality was an unwritten cultural expectation of the ancient Near East. Abraham killed the fatted calf—the best he could offer—for his guests (Genesis 18:6-8). Similarly, Lot prepared dinner for two angelic guests (Genesis 19:3). Joseph treated his brutalizing brothers to a banquet when they arrived from a famine-stricken land (Genesis 43:24-34).

INTERACTIVE IDEA

Have individuals turn to one other person and describe their favorite food or meal.

WHAT TO SAY

In the world-famous Psalm 23, the psalmist, David, affirms that God prepares a table for him (Psalm 23:5). Rather than *condescending* to David, the Almighty *caters* to David's desires.

This is no ordinary banquet. Our Lover takes us into his "banquet hall" (Song of Songs 2:4). The King is at his table (Song of Songs 1:12). In effect, we're offered queenly treatment as honored guests.

"The wine how rich, the bread how sweet,

When Jesus deigns the guests to meet!"

—Charles Spurgeon

In the Last Supper, the Lord announced that he would drink again someday with his own in his Father's kingdom (Matthew 26:29). Therefore, we await our personalized invitation to the "wedding supper of the Lamb" (Revelation 19:9).

Meanwhile, the bread and the cup that we take here are merely a foretaste of the future feast when we will meet to eat at the banquet table of our King.

Do you ever try to envision that futuristic celebration? How do you see your role there? Does it motivate you in your present life? Do you want to have any rewards—as 2 Timothy 4:8 offers—to present in appreciation to the Lord, your banquet host?

As we partake now of this mini-banquet, let's be mindful of the vastly greater banquet to come.

Beauty in the Eye of the Beholder
Scripture: Psalm 27:4

▼ ▼ ▼ ▼ ▼ ▼ ▼ ▼ ▼ ▼ ▼ ▼ ▼ ▼ ▼ ▼ ▼ ▼

WHAT TO SAY

The poet Keats wrote, "A thing of beauty is a joy forever." Our world is enamored of outward physical beauty. Beauty attracts us. We long to look at the beautiful.

The psalmist wanted "to gaze upon the beauty of the Lord" (Psalm 27:4). Certainly all the glittering gold and white marble and cloistered colonnades of the Jerusalem Temple would have dazzled the eyes of the beholder with its external beauty.

The splendor of the Temple was intended to induce God's people to behold the Lord with the eyes of the heart. How do we do that? We start by valuing the things God values and treasuring things of real worth. Not by *sight* but by *insight* into God's worth do we come to greater appreciation of the beauty of all God's attributes.

Just as outer beauty draws us to look, so God's Spirit draws us to "gaze upon the beauty of the Lord" through his invitation to the Lord's table. Isaiah 53:2 says of the Messiah, "He had no beauty or majesty to attract us to him."

Similarly, there is no outward beauty in a morsel of bread or a sip from a cup. Yet our faith provides insight into who Christ is and what he's done for us. We can see beyond the bread and cup something vastly beautiful beyond our comprehension.

As you take part in communion today, "gaze upon the beauty of the Lord."

The Multi-Titled Messiah
Scripture: Isaiah 9:6

▼ ▼ ▼ ▼ ▼ ▼ ▼ ▼ ▼ ▼ ▼ ▼ ▼ ▼ ▼ ▼ ▼

USE THE UNUSUAL

Play the portion of Handel's "Messiah" that begins with words from Isaiah 9:6: "Wonderful, counselor." Have your sound technician begin the piece at full volume and then fade to background music while you give the message.

INTERACTIVE IDEA

In staccato fashion—each saying just three or four words—members of the congregation can share benefits of knowing Christ or words they would use to describe him.

WHAT TO SAY

Even those who are dyed-in-the-wool musical lowbrows often recognize the strains of Handel's "Messiah." One of the most memorable sections announces some of the qualities of our multifaceted Messiah. In Isaiah 9:6 we encounter Christ's

- *psychological* capacity as "wonderful counselor." How many of us are like Woody Allen, who has spent thousands on psychoanalysis? Why not turn to the enabling and empowering "wonderful Counselor"?
- *power,* for he is "mighty God." The Old Testament directly declares the deity of the coming Messiah.
- *paternity.* This title must mystify many. How can the eternal Son be an "everlasting Father"? Did Isaiah mix up the persons of the Trinity? No. Some scholars have suggested he is the one who, we might say, fathered eternity. Besides, as the perfect image of God the Father (Hebrews 1:3), **God the Son mirrors the character of the Father** (John 1:18; 14:9).
- *peace.* Christians receive the bequest of Christ's peace (John 16:33).

As participants at the Lord's table, all the beautiful benefits are ours. All that he represents—in the titles of Isaiah 9:6—is channeled to us as we take it into ourselves. Eating at communion is a simple, yet dramatic, way of saying, "I take all that Christ is into me."

Behind God's Back
Scripture: Isaiah 38:17

▼ ▼ ▼ ▼ ▼ ▼ ▼ ▼ ▼ ▼ ▼ ▼ ▼ ▼ ▼ ▼ ▼

INTERACTIVE IDEA

Ask members of your congregation to gather in groups of six or so and come up with word pictures from the modern world that might serve as depictions of forgiveness. Ask a selected person from each group to share the group's images of pardon with the entire congregation.

WHAT TO SAY

A picture, so it's said, is worth a thousand words. The Old Testament offers two masterpieces in its gallery that represent the fullness of God's forgiveness.

First, the speaker in Isaiah 38:17 states, "You [God], have put all my sins behind your back." Think about it—your sins are hidden behind the greatness of God. This is God's way of announcing, "Your sins are *gone!*"

A second picture of pardon is found in Micah 7:19—our sins are hurled out into the depths of the ocean. While Satan might try to be a deep-sea diver and discover incriminating evidence against us, our sins are buried beyond all boundaries, for God had dissolved them.

Behind God's back and "buried in the deepest sea; yes, that's good enough for me. Praise God, my sins are...gone!"

What an introduction to taking communion! Think of your rottenness, your wrongs, your disobedience staring you in the face. How can you dispose of them? God says, "Pretend I have a back; now put your sins behind me where they'll never be seen again. If that's not enough, I'll also take those same sins and sink them in the sea."

Who Was That Masked Man?
Scripture: Isaiah 53:2

▼ ▼ ▼ ▼ ▼ ▼ ▼ ▼ ▼ ▼ ▼ ▼ ▼ ▼ ▼ ▼ ▼ ▼

INTERACTIVE IDEA

Senior adults in your congregation might enjoy naming movie cowboys from the past. Ask them to describe in just a sentence or two the qualities they liked about their favorites.

WHAT TO SAY

He arrived with his identity masked. However, there was little mistaking the powder-blue pants and shirt highlighted by the red bandanna and white hat. Even more identifiable were the black mask, silver bullets, and the great white stallion named Silver. Who was that masked man? Why, he was the Lone Ranger, played on TV by Clayton Moore.

Earlier in the movies, another masked rider thrilled youngsters. He wore all black and had a black bandanna covering the lower half of his face like an outlaw, while he rode his great white steed, Raider. He was the Durango Kid.

These two movie and TV cowboys looked like bad guys because their identities were masked.

Who expected a Messiah with a masked identity? Yes, the Messiah for the nations arrived in disguise. The prophets had predicted it. He wasn't physically attractive (Isaiah 53:2). He didn't fit the expected profile of a champion. He didn't campaign against the hated Roman conquerors. And he also was treated as an outlaw (Isaiah 53:12).

Christ's significance is hidden from many people. Yet, believers grasp the identity of the person inside the simple exterior.

Just as grains were crushed by a millstone, Christ was crushed beneath our sins. Just as wine was made by crushing grapes, so Christ experienced the full weight of our wrongs. We Christians have profound appreciation for him because we recognize and acknowledge his true identity.

Duncan Renaldo and Our Lord
Scripture: Isaiah 53:3-8

▼ ▼ ▼ ▼ ▼ ▼ ▼ ▼ ▼ ▼ ▼ ▼ ▼ ▼ ▼ ▼ ▼ ▼

OBJECT LESSON

Ask a creative person in your congregation to put together a mural or collage of visual samples of racism or oppression. You might find ideas for images in magazines, on the Internet, or in library books on the civil rights movement. Because he was oppressed, Jesus relates to all oppressed peoples of the world.

WHAT TO SAY

Maybe you've never heard of Duncan Renaldo, but I want to talk for a minute about the raw deal he got. Evidently, he was the victim of racism.

Renaldo landed a part in a Hollywood film in 1929. Yet at the premiere of *Trader Horn*, at the famous Grauman's Chinese Theater, he was arrested as an illegal immigrant. For six years, he was hauled into courtrooms on the charge. He actually served a year and a half in prison. Finally, President Franklin Roosevelt granted Renaldo an unconditional pardon.

Renaldo had to start all over again by sweeping floors at Republic Studios. To his credit, studio head Herbert Yates put Renaldo back in the saddle again. Finally Duncan Renaldo got his biggest break when he starred as the Cisco Kid on more than 150 thirty-minute TV shows.

Isaiah paints a similar portrait of our rejected Messiah. "He was despised" (Isaiah 53:3). "He was oppressed" (Isaiah 53:7). "By oppression…he was taken away" (Isaiah 53:8). He suffered unjustly for what he'd never done.

Ultimately Christ was reinstated. The charges were reversed. The victim became the victor. We celebrate him due to and despite his rejection. In communion, the bread speaks of his brutalization. The fruit of the vine reminds us of his outpoured offering. He is our honored hero, and God the Father has raised him to the highest heaven.

He for Me
Scripture: Isaiah 53:5-6

▼ ▼ ▼ ▼ ▼ ▼ ▼ ▼ ▼ ▼ ▼ ▼ ▼ ▼ ▼ ▼ ▼ ▼

INTERACTIVE IDEA

Ask everyone present to turn to another person and share an example of a *substitute*. For example, a baseball manager might use a substitute runner or pinch hitter in a critical inning. A sick teacher might need a substitute.

WHAT TO SAY

Did you ever serve as a substitute for someone? Have you ever filled in for someone, completing the tasks he or she ordinarily would be expected to accomplish?

Isaiah 53:5-6 is a classic passage that illustrates the "he-for-me" doctrine in the Bible.

> **"He was pierced for our transgressions,**
> **he was crushed for our iniquities...**
> **and the Lord has laid on him**
> **the iniquity of us all."**

The theological term for "he-for-me" is *substitutionary atonement*. But rather than get overly doctrinal, we can make this a very personal statement by changing the pronouns in this passage from Isaiah from *us* and *our* to *I* and *me*.

***I* deserved punishment. Jesus absorbed *my* punishment. Now he presents *me* with the offer of paradise.**

It's he-for-me. Paul echoed this truth in 1 Corinthians 15:3: "Christ died for our sins." He took our sins. And in communion we remember his work as a substitute.

***I* take the bread and the cup and remember that he died for *me*.**

Old Testament Salvation Scripture: Isaiah 53:11

▼ ▼ ▼ ▼ ▼ ▼ ▼ ▼ ▼ ▼ ▼ ▼ ▼ ▼ ▼ ▼ ▼ ▼

INTERACTIVE IDEA

Ask worshippers to turn to someone near them and ask each other, "What would you like to know about me that you don't know?" Give everyone a few minutes to participate in this way.

WHAT TO SAY

If you wanted to show a Jewish inquirer a simple "salvation verse," what might it be? If it is translated as one Hebrew scholar suggested, no verse may be clearer than Isaiah 53:11. The text may be rendered as "My servant as a righteous one will justify" (Edward J. Young, *The Book of Isaiah*).

Acts 8:32-35 unmistakably links the suffering servant of Isaiah 53 with Jesus. In Acts 8, a Jewish Christian had just quoted Isaiah 53:7-8 to a non-Christian African and identified the person the passage speaks of as Jesus. The job of Jesus as suffering servant was to justify many (Romans 5:15). God, as Supreme Court justice of the universe, can acquit the guilty because Jesus died for us, the unjust.

How are we acquitted? How do we come through the entrance gate? The answer is "by knowing him." To "know" God through Christ is the definition of having eternal life in John 17:3. All who believe—that is, all who receive Christ—have eternal life (John 1:12).

Do you know Christ? All who know him personally by faith are freely invited to partake together in communion. Today, if you receive Christ by faith personally into your life, you are ready to receive communion because now you truly know him.

Where the Grapes of Wrath Are Stored
Scripture: Isaiah 63:1-6

▼ ▼ ▼ ▼ ▼ ▼ ▼ ▼ ▼ ▼ ▼ ▼ ▼ ▼ ▼ ▼ ▼

BACKGROUND

John Steinbeck authored a significant book titled *The Grapes of Wrath*. The title comes from the Civil War hymn "Battle Hymn of the Republic." The well-known lines of this hymn announce that God "is trampling out the vintage where the *grapes of wrath* are stored."

This moving picture comes from Isaiah 63:1-6 and Revelation 14:17-20. The one depicted in Isaiah 63:1-3 is a figure with his robe-ends splattered from grape-trampling—much in the manner a modern person would jump up and down on a trampoline. "Why are your garments red?" asks the anonymous questioner in Isaiah 63:2.

WHAT TO SAY

At the cross of Calvary, Christ drank down to the dregs the cup of God's wrath (Mark 10:38). He treaded the winepress of God's wrath over sin. In effect, our blood spattered his garments (Isaiah 63:3).

Christ imbibed our cup of guilt so that we might share his cup of grace. While his was the bitter cup of brutality, we drink from a shared cup of blessing. He trampled "the winepress alone" (Isaiah 63:3). Why? Our sins sent him there. We are the cause of his crucifixion.

The *bread* we break—even as his body was pulverized—and the *cup* we drink, which stands for his outpoured life, vividly portray these truths.

So grasp. Share. Drink. Remember.

Splendor and Shame
Scripture: Ezekiel 1

▼ ▼ ▼ ▼ ▼ ▼ ▼ ▼ ▼ ▼ ▼ ▼ ▼ ▼ ▼ ▼ ▼ ▼

INTERACTIVE IDEA

Have people turn to someone else and share the first word that comes to mind when they hear the word *glory.*

WHAT TO SAY

[As you begin, read aloud Ezekiel 1:4-28, highlighting the words *like* and *appearance.*] **Ezekiel had amazing visions of God** (Ezekiel 1:1). **Later, Ezekiel also underwent significant shame** (as Ezekiel 4:12-15 and 5:1-4 indicate). **In fact, in Hebrew, his name can mean "God strengthens" or it can mean "God makes hard." While he had a vision of God, he also was the subject of scoffing and shame, as was our Savior** (Isaiah 53:3).

When you think of catching a glimpse of God's glory, do you think of Christ on the cross? The cross seems anything but a place of glory, honor, or splendor. Yet Christ's dishonor has become our honor. Because he lowered himself to shame and sacrifice, God the Father crowned him with glory and honor (Hebrews 2:9).

When we carry out his command concerning communion, we honor him for the shame he suffered for us. It honors him and gives him glory.

A Whale of a Time!
Scripture: Jonah 2:1-7

▼ ▼ ▼ ▼ ▼ ▼ ▼ ▼ ▼ ▼ ▼ ▼ ▼ ▼ ▼ ▼ ▼ ▼ ▼

OBJECT LESSON

Hold up a picture of a whale, or display a copy of the classic book *Moby Dick* as you begin.

WHAT TO SAY

One of American literature's great classics is the early chapter in Herman Melville's *Moby Dick* when Father Mapple preaches a sermon to the Nantucket mariners about Jonah. The old sailor-turned-preacher uses the story of Jonah to warn his listeners who are about to ship out.

Anyone who has ever worried about drowning can relate to Jonah's deep-sea, near-drowning experience. "Help!" is the frantic cry of anyone who is drowning. Jonah later described his underwater experience as if he were going down to the grave (Jonah 2:2). He was swallowed in "the very heart of the seas" (2:3). He could say to God, "all your waves and breakers swept over me" (2:3).

Jonah is like Jesus in some ways. In fact, the Hebrew text of Jonah 2:2 takes Jonah down to *Sheol.* This is the same thing Peter said of Jesus in Acts 2:27—he went down to *Sheol* or "the grave." Yet, like Jonah, Jesus emerged from the grave to new life.

Our Lord spoke of his upcoming experience of death as if it were an underwater experience of drowning—a "baptism" (Mark 10:38). His human life was temporarily snuffed out, because he died for our sins (1 Corinthians 15:3).

The claustrophobic, suffocating reality of his death enables us to enter appreciatively into the depth of his "drowning." If you've ever felt that you were drowning, you can relate somewhat to Jesus' feelings when God's "waves and breakers swept over" him on the cross (Jonah 2:3). He sank beneath the load of our crimes.

We take in communion because Jesus took in our sins. It's our way of entering mentally into what he entered into physically.

USE THE UNUSUAL

If you know of someone who's had a near-drowning experience, ask if that person would be willing to describe his or her sensations before you begin the meditation.

Blessed by a Translation Error?
Scripture: Haggai 2:7

▼ ▼ ▼ ▼ ▼ ▼ ▼ ▼ ▼ ▼ ▼ ▼ ▼ ▼ ▼ ▼ ▼ ▼

USE THE UNUSUAL

Introduce this meditation by asking someone who has been through a rough earthquake to recall his or her experience.

OBJECT LESSON

Try to get a videotape of game three of the 1989 World Series between Oakland and San Francisco, and show part of it to your congregation. It's not the game you will care about showing. Instead, you'll want to show that just as this game was about to start, the screen goes blank as a 7.1-magnitude earthquake hit the Bay Area and ultimately took the lives of sixty-seven people.

WHAT TO SAY

Haggai was an Old Testament spokesperson who carried a message of doom and gloom. He announced a *heavenquake* (Haggai 2:6). Then Haggai—echoing God's voice—announced, "I will shake all nations, and the desired of all nations will come" (2:7). In Haggai's ambiguous expression, the "desired" he's describing is plural, so it probably refers contextually to the silver and gold of Haggai 2:8, the very next verse. In other words, in the future, very desirable treasure would be brought to God's temple.

On the basis of the King James translation of verse 7, Charles Wesley borrowed the phrase as a title for Christ—the "desire of nations." Wesley penned "Come, Desire of nations, come." It is one of the less-familiar stanzas of the very familiar Christmas carol "Hark, the Herald Angels Sing."

Do the nations desire Christ? Certainly around God's throne will be people from every people-group and nation (Revelation 5:9). Yet many reject him too. Still, God has set eternal yearnings in the human heart (Ecclesiastes 3:11).

All who truly desire the Desire of Nations will find him. And he desires to commune with us as we partake of the bread and cup.

Zechariah's Pen-Portrait
Scripture: Zechariah 9:9

▼ ▼ ▼ ▼ ▼ ▼ ▼ ▼ ▼ ▼ ▼ ▼ ▼ ▼ ▼ ▼ ▼ ▼

INTERACTIVE IDEA

Ahead of time, ask some children in your church about their experiences with horses (the horses' names and colors and the children's experiences with them). Choose children with colorful stories, and briefly interview them.

WHAT TO SAY

Five hundred years before Jesus appeared as a human in the world, a spokesperson named Zechariah sketched a verbal picture of what Jesus would be like. Zechariah announced that this coming One would arrive in Jerusalem astride an unbroken donkey (Zechariah 9:9; Mark 11:2).

Zechariah also said this future One would be pierced (Zechariah 12:10) **and wounded treacherously among his own friends** (Zechariah 13:6). **Half a millennium later, this is exactly what happened to Jesus.**

Zechariah announced that someday "the Lord will be king over the whole earth" (Zechariah 14:9) **and that "his rule will extend from sea to sea"** (Zechariah 9:10). **We don't see everything on planet Earth under Christ's control right now** (Hebrews 2:8), **but that is a faith aspect of our future that we subscribe to when we take communion. Jesus indicated that we celebrate communion "until he comes"** (1 Corinthians 11:26).

As we think about Zechariah and his future depiction of Jesus, we take communion with the anticipation of a magnificent future shared with Christ. Let this mentally sink in as you partake of communion today.

Chapter 4
Ministry of Jesus:
Meditations From the Gospels

The Man for All Seasons

Lights Out!

Two Kisses

Incomprehensible Incarnation

I Love You

Our Christmas Carol

E.T.

By George!

The Spirit as Stagehand

Trampled!

Silent Speakers

The Man for All Seasons
Scripture: Mark 15:9-11

▼ ▼ ▼ ▼ ▼ ▼ ▼ ▼ ▼ ▼ ▼ ▼ ▼ ▼ ▼ ▼ ▼

BACKGROUND

The title of the movie *A Man for All Seasons* seems to suggest that some people are born to accomplish things as ideal individuals. They seem larger than life.

Long ago, writers created Everyman plays. In these plays we see ourselves and qualities we all possess. In fact, all great literature is really aimed at getting every one of us into the act—that is, seeing our attitudes and actions emerging in the characters we read about.

INTERACTIVE IDEA

Ask each person to turn to someone other than a family member and, after you give them a minute to think it through, tell how they've seen something of themselves in someone else (for example, a tendency to finish someone else's sentences or a propensity to shy away from conflict).

WHAT TO SAY

Barabbas was a kind of Everyman. His very name signified that he was a "son (bar) of a father (abba)." Barabbas was a violator of laws (Mark 15:7). So are we. We've violated God's laws. We are Barabbases. We have rebelled—only ours is an insurrection against high heaven.

Barabbas should have died for his crimes, yet he was given a substitute. He may have looked up at the center cross at Calvary and thought, "I should've been there, but he died in my place."

You are Barabbas. You deserved death; you are a bona fide rebel, yet Christ spared you from death because he died for you. Since Jesus is God, he is great enough to die for everyone. In a sense, he is the ultimate Everyman.

Communion reminds us that Christ died for us. Remember him. He made the all-embracing sacrifice. He died for you and you and you. When we take communion today, we're thanking him that he included each of us in his all-inclusive death.

Lights Out!
Scripture: Mark 15:33

▼ ▼ ▼ ▼ ▼ ▼ ▼ ▼ ▼ ▼ ▼ ▼ ▼ ▼ ▼ ▼ ▼ ▼

USE THE UNUSUAL

Make your auditorium as dark as you can during your meditation and communion time. After communion, light a single candle at the front of your auditorium, noting how this single source of light can illuminate a whole room.

WHAT TO SAY

Have you ever been in an underground cavern, such as Carlsbad Caverns or Mammoth Cave, when the guides turned out all the lights? It's the darkest of the dark. The guides claim that eventually people in such extreme darkness will lose their vision and, after a number of weeks, their sanity!

Remember that as Jesus was dying, God enveloped the earth in darkness for three hours (Mark 15:33). It was as if a giant hand had suddenly switched off the lights of the universe.

One poet, imagining that scene, suggested that the sun saw her Maker crucified—and blushed! As Isaac Watts put it:

"Well might the sun in darkness hide

And shut [Christ's] glories in,

When the Incarnate Maker died

For man, His creature's sin."

When the Light of the world died, all the lights went out! That darkness symbolized the blight of humanity as sin-darkened creatures, wandering in lostness. Christ is the light of the world (John 8:12). When we come to him, we enter the light of life.

Communion causes Christians to reflect on their dark pasts and what might have been if Christ's light hadn't flooded in on them.

Two Kisses
Scripture: Luke 15:20

▼ ▼ ▼ ▼ ▼ ▼ ▼ ▼ ▼ ▼ ▼ ▼ ▼ ▼ ▼ ▼ ▼ ▼

USE THE UNUSUAL

Ask a married couple to cross in front of the congregation, each entering from opposite sides, pausing in the middle to kiss, and then exiting together.

WHAT TO SAY

Movie screens are awash with famous kisses—including the classic scene of a couple bidding farewell as one is about to board a plane for a faraway place.

Let's go back to a scene of long ago: Envision a heartbroken father relentlessly scanning the horizon, seeking a silhouette so familiar to him. Finally, one day, a spot on the horizon causes the Jewish elder to squint and reignite his hopes. He blinks his eyes until...finally, he realizes it's true. "It's my boy!" The dignified elder drops all pretenses of protocol as he races down the road toward the ragged returnee. The prodigal father ("prodigal" can mean he was lavish in his generosity) smothers the young man in kisses (Luke 15:20).

This scene is merely the mirror of God's own graciousness when he welcomes us home to him. An old hymn by James Deck says, "Thou thy prodigals hast pardoned, 'kissed us' with a father's love."

Kisses are tokens of affection. The bread and the cup are tokens of Christ's love. In a sense they're like packaged kisses from him to us. When we take communion, we're returning affection to God. We "kiss the Son" (Psalm 2:12). We express our adoration and affection toward the Lord—like reciprocating kisses—when we please him by receiving the two tokens of affection he offers us.

Incomprehensible Incarnation
Scripture: John 1:14

▼ ▼ ▼ ▼ ▼ ▼ ▼ ▼ ▼ ▼ ▼ ▼ ▼ ▼ ▼ ▼ ▼ ▼

USE THE UNUSUAL

If you have a skilled mime in your congregation, ask him or her to perform a mime in preparation for this meditation. The mime will do the classic mime bit—pretending that a small room is closing in on him or her. The enclosure gets smaller and smaller. As the person freezes on stage, ask, "What would it be like for the one in whom the universe exists (as Acts 17:28 declares) to move into the confines of his own universe, contracted into a single human form?"

WHAT TO SAY

In the 1700s, Charles Wesley penned these lines concerning Christ's incarnation:

"Our God contracted to a span,

Incomprehensibly made man."

Imagine an elephant being "contracted" to the point that it fits inside a thimble, and you begin to understand what Charles Wesley was saying. The eternal Son of God was reduced in form to a human body.

A relative once asked a pastor what was the most profound idea he'd heard from any of his many teachers. At first his mind immediately froze. Then, since it was Christmastime, he remembered: Immanuel, meaning "God with us." The eternal God in fleshly, human form surely is the most remarkable reality we can know. Imagine that the One who made the universe was reduced to the wobbliness of a toddler!

Eternity was embodied in an earthly envelope. We celebrate this every time we receive communion. We hear the echo "This is my body, my blood given for you." Surely if God's Son offered himself for you, in return you can offer yourself to him in loving service, in courageous acts, in kindly compassion. That's the "So what?" of God's embodiment in humanity. Now you are to embody God's love to someone else this week.

"My body, my blood…for you. Take.

Remember me."

I Love You
Scripture: John 21:17

▼ ▼ ▼ ▼ ▼ ▼ ▼ ▼ ▼ ▼ ▼ ▼ ▼ ▼ ▼ ▼ ▼ ▼

WHAT TO SAY

Good old blundering, blustering Peter. Open-mouth, insert-foot Peter. Wow! The stuff he said. Remember his immortal quote: "No...you shall never wash my feet" (John 13:8). That immediately preceded his 180-degree change of direction when he essentially said, "Lord, give me the whole-body bath."

So, Peter got a grilling in John 21:15-17 by his friend who had come back from the dead. Must have been embarrassing—to be asked virtually the same question—"Simon, do you love me?"—three times in a row, in front of all his friends.

How many times have we, like Peter, flunked our spiritual assignments? How many times have we botched it when we were thrust into a precarious situation? In any case, despite his denial, Peter remained immovable in his ardent affirmation: "Lord, you know all things; you know that I love you" (John 21:17).

We often come to the communion table with a conscience that silently screams at us, "You've blown it again...and again...and again." Yet in the overwhelming presence of his love, we meekly mumble, "I love you." As we take communion today, we say to him, "Lord, you know all things—including my failures. But you also know that I love you."

Our Christmas Carol
Scripture: 1 Timothy 3:16

▼ ▼ ▼ ▼ ▼ ▼ ▼ ▼ ▼ ▼ ▼ ▼ ▼ ▼ ▼ ▼ ▼ ▼

WHAT TO SAY

A famous Christmas carol unloads boxcars full of truth on us. It says of Christ:

> *"Veiled in flesh, the Godhead see;*
> *Hail, the incarnate Deity:*
> *Pleased, as man, with men to dwell,*
> *Jesus, our Emmanuel!"*
> —Charles Wesley

[Hold up a facial tissue.] **Take a look at this tissue. It might remind you of the face veils worn by women in Middle Eastern countries. The song-writer indicated in these lines that Christ's "Godhead" was "veiled in flesh." First Timothy 3:16 says, "He appeared in a body." Paul considered this a huge mystery.**

This familiar Christmas carol isn't just a little ditty; it's packed with theological truth. The word *incarnate* is related in form to words like *carnal, carnival,* or even chili con *carne* (that is, chili with meat or "flesh"). That the God of the universe reduced himself to the cramped, confined condition of our flesh—that's the great truth of Christmas.

We celebrate not only at Christmas that God has become incarnate, we also celebrate that here each time we partake of communion. Jesus is "our Emmanuel," which means "God with us." God is present with us here in communion.

Just as Christ's body was the material embodiment of his love, so he's provided the bread and cup as material, tangible expressions of his love for us.

E.T.
Scripture: 2 Corinthians 8:9

▼ ▼ ▼ ▼ ▼ ▼ ▼ ▼ ▼ ▼ ▼ ▼ ▼ ▼ ▼ ▼ ▼ ▼

BACKGROUND

Christ voluntarily became poor for us, but we richly share his heavenly wealth in communion.

INTERACTIVE IDEA

After about a half minute for reflection, have each person turn to someone else and indicate one very specific expectation they might have if they were very poor (such as scrounging in garbage cans for food).

WHAT TO SAY

The initials E.T. became enshrined in American linguistic usage through the introduction of a movie bearing that two-letter name. *E.T.* in the movie means "extraterrestrial." The movie depicts a creature who visits our planet from outer space.

But have you ever stopped to consider that another E.T. had long ago invaded planet Earth? Second Corinthians 8:9 declared of Christ, "Though he was rich, yet for your sakes he became poor."

One individual inquired concerning Christ's stay on planet Earth, "When was he ever rich?" Since Jesus, as God the Son, had eternally enjoyed with God the Father all of heaven's riches, he could be clearly described as "rich." Christ is the answer to the riddle "Who lived before he was *born*?" Paul's proclamation presupposes Christ's pre-existence, for he was never "rich" on earth. He was rich as the "E.T.," sharing equally in God the Father's glory (John 5:18; 17:5).

Yet, at the same time, Jesus was essentially a Palestinian peasant during his sojourn here on earth. He was the poorest of the poor. He willingly shared himself with us, to the point of giving up his Father's riches and living in poverty. What he did for us was purely voluntary. Once we genuinely grasp Christ's volunteering for a life of poverty and a death of agony, we can take communion with a new sense of the wonder of it all.

By George!
Scripture: John 15:1

▼ ▼ ▼ ▼ ▼ ▼ ▼ ▼ ▼ ▼ ▼ ▼ ▼ ▼ ▼ ▼ ▼ ▼

USE THE UNUSUAL

Ask an amateur gardener in your congregation to talk briefly about a few of his or her favorite flowers or plants. Or briefly interview this person, leading him or her to talk about the effort that goes into making plants grow.

WHAT TO SAY

George Washington, George Washington Carver, two George Bushes, Curious George (the monkey in children's literature), and even Gorgeous George (the wrestler of 1950s notoriety)! The name *George* is certainly a familiar one, but its Greek-oriented use in the New Testament is not nearly so familiar.

It's a little hard for us to picture God as a George! But in John 15:1, the Greek form of our derived name George is found behind the more familiar term "gardener." In John 15:1, Jesus announced that God the Father is our gardener. The Greek term is pronounced *geh-ohr-GAHSS*. This would be spelled out (or transliterated) *georgos,* which includes five of the six letters in the American name George.

What we do in gardening (planting, tending, caring, weeding, pruning, harvesting, and so on), God does for us in a much more elevated sense. God's people are his plants.

What kind of germination and growth is happening at this season in your life? This should be one of the things we reflect on as we approach communion, for we've been invited to partake in a worthy manner (1 Corinthians 11:27). Reflect in this moment of quiet contemplation upon how you might function as a more "worthy" garden plot this week, allowing God to do his spading and fertilizing in your life. Then take the bread and cup from your divine Gardener.

The Spirit as Stagehand
Scripture: John 16:13

▼ ▼ ▼ ▼ ▼ ▼ ▼ ▼ ▼ ▼ ▼ ▼ ▼ ▼ ▼ ▼ ▼ ▼

INTERACTIVE IDEA

Have people cluster in groups of three and share for a few moments about times they felt the glare of the public limelight focused upon them (perhaps in a school play or recital or in embarrassment).

WHAT TO SAY

"Lights! Camera! Action!" So commands the movie director—at least in the movies. But nothing that happened on the set would ever be known if it weren't for another anonymous person—the cameraman. It is his duty to place the stars in the limelight. Similarly, as the main actor steps out onto center stage, someone in the wings of the theater has directed that person into the floodlights. Another anonymous person—or many people—have made sure the lights actually work and are aimed in the right direction.

In John 16:13, Jesus states that the Spirit of God would glorify the Son of God. One of the main roles—perhaps the paramount role—of the Spirit of God is to shine the stage lights upon the Son of God. The Holy Spirit has been called the "shy person" of the Trinity, taking on a backstage, behind-the-curtains role. It certainly seems that he works that way. For example, we don't see him working in our lives, but we sense that he is present and active within us.

In communion, the principal honoree is God's Son. Some see him as both the host who invites us to his table (Mark 14:22) and the guest who receives our recognition and reverence. We remember *him*—as he has asked us and as he accordingly deserves our adoration. He is deity; therefore, he deserves our devotion. He died for us; therefore, how can we not respond with reciprocating love?

As we thank him for his tender treatment, we're aware that it is the Spirit of God in us who promotes the Son of God among us. If we're honoring the Son of God, the Holy Spirit is content because he's accomplished his principal purpose.

Trampled!
Scripture: John 18:1

▼ ▼ ▼ ▼ ▼ ▼ ▼ ▼ ▼ ▼ ▼ ▼ ▼ ▼ ▼ ▼ ▼

OBJECT LESSON

A Bible dictionary or encyclopedia might contain pictures of ancient olive presses. Ask an artistic person in your congregation to draw a large picture of one as a visual aid. Or if you have a projection system, simply display a drawing on your screen.

WHAT TO SAY

On his last night as a human on this planet, Jesus entered into an olive grove (John 18:1). Somewhere nearby would have been an olive press. An olive press looked a bit like a split-level, connected pair of stone bathtubs. Olive oil would drain from the upper tub into the lower vat as individuals trampled on the olives in the olive press.

The olive press at Gethsemane carried a vastly deeper significance. That night in the garden, it was as if our sins were trampling Christ. We trampled him. To borrow a phrase from Hebrews 10:29, our sins "trampled the Son of God under foot." We drained the very life out of him at Calvary. We were his violators. We caused his death.

Christ died for each of us—for me, for you. But because we have accepted that atoning work when we accepted him as Savior, we can say thank you in an emphatic way. That's what we do when we take the bread (the body that we broke) and the cup (the blood that we spilt). Do this in remembrance—and in thankfulness—of him.

Silent Speakers
Scripture: Luke 19:40

▼ ▼ ▼ ▼ ▼ ▼ ▼ ▼ ▼ ▼ ▼ ▼ ▼ ▼ ▼ ▼ ▼ ▼

WHAT TO SAY

As Jesus made his heart-rending, final entry into Jerusalem during the last week of his ministry on earth, he met with the equivalent of a ticker-tape parade: "The whole crowd of disciples began joyfully to praise God in loud voices" (Luke 19:37). It was a singularly moving moment.

In that dramatic moment, however, he also slammed headlong into opposition. His outright enemies reprimanded him, wanting him to silence his disciples (Luke 19:39). Yet Jesus retorted, "If they keep quiet, the stones will cry out" (Luke 19:40).

Shouting stones! Wow, there's an oxymoron, a contradiction of terms. Yet our world is chock-full of nonverbal communications.

I once heard the story of a new pastor who went for the first time to a nursing home to visit a man whose mental faculties were virtually gone. The pastor introduced himself. When he mentioned the church, tears welled up in the old man's eyes. Although the elderly man spoke no words, he took the pastor's hand, brought it up to his lips, and kissed it. What an unforgettable example of nonverbal communication!

Here on this table before us are two nonverbal communicators. They say to you: Like bread-grains being crushed, Christ gave up his body for you. Like liquid poured from this cup, Christ poured out his blood for you. Let him express his lavish love to you as you partake of the elements, as if he were here handing them to you individually.

USE THE UNUSUAL

When you're speaking the words in the final paragraph of the meditation, you can take a piece of bread or crackers and crush them in your hands. Similarly, take the cup and pour a bit of the contents on the communion table.

Chapter 5
Salvation and Righteousness:
Meditations From Romans

The Interceptor

Our Double Defense

Softness and Severity

Unfathomable Depths

The Interceptor
Scripture: Romans 3:25

▼ ▼ ▼ ▼ ▼ ▼ ▼ ▼ ▼ ▼ ▼ ▼ ▼ ▼ ▼ ▼ ▼ ▼ ▼

USE THE UNUSUAL

Draft several high-school students to mime or run a slow-motion football play. The quarterback takes the hike from the center. Then the receiver goes for the pass in slow motion. However, the defensive back steps in and intercepts the pass.

WHAT TO SAY

The score seems settled. The winning team has the football and is heading in the right direction toward the opponents' end zone. They're ahead by three points. Less than one minute left to play. Then it happens. The quarterback tosses what seems like a certain completion. But then from out of nowhere a defensive back *intercepts* the ball, runs down the field, and crosses his goal line. In the last second, the other team pulls out an upset.

Intercept, intervene, interpose—all these "inter" words contain the Latin-derived root meaning "in between." Just as a defensive player steps in between the ball and the intended receiver, so Christ stands between us and God. In Romans 3:25 Paul pictured Christ as our go-between.

In Tabernacle terminology, he's our mercy seat or atoning sacrifice. In between a shimmeringly perfect God and a sinningly imperfect people stood the Tabernacle's mercy seat. Atoning blood sacrifice was the in-between factor.

We were headed toward the wrong goal line in life, but Christ *intervened* on our behalf. He *interposed* his precious blood. He *intercepted* our hellish destiny. Now he *intercedes* for all his people (Romans 8:34). As we enter into his "interception," we commune with him.

Thank God today for our mediator (1 Timothy 2:5) who stands between God and our sin. Remember his intervention. The bread and cup speak of the death he died on our behalf. Take communion and reflect on Christ's intervention for you.

Our Double Defense
Scripture: Romans 8:16; 1 John 2:2

▼ ▼ ▼ ▼ ▼ ▼ ▼ ▼ ▼ ▼ ▼ ▼ ▼ ▼ ▼ ▼ ▼ ▼ ▼

USE THE UNUSUAL

Check with a number of trusted friends to see who has had an accusation (preferably an unfounded or bizarre one) made against them. After ensuring that sharing such an accusation publicly will affect absolutely no one in your congregation, ask one person to describe the experience to the congregation.

WHAT TO SAY

In the story of the woman taken in adultery, Jesus asked her afterward, "Woman, where are [your accusers]?" (John 8:10). She replied that there were no viable or visible accusers. Romans 8:33 asks who will accuse God's chosen ones. The rhetorical answer is "no one."

Revelation 12:10 dubs the devil as the Christian's "accuser." In essence, he's the prosecutor in the case against us. Thankfully, however, we have a double defense, consisting of

• the Son of God, who defends us in heaven (1 John 2:2), and

• the Spirit of God, who defends us in our hearts (Romans 8:16).

Scripture uses the Greek word *parakletos* [pah-RAH-klay-tahss] when referring to both Son and Spirit. They champion our cause. These co-lawyers have their case grounded in Christ's cross. On the cross, the sentence has already been served. Therefore, justice has been served. The accused become the acquitted. We are free. The Spirit answers to Christ's blood and tells us we are born of God (see Romans 8:16).

Therefore, the one who died for you defends you even now. If we stood alone and on our own before God as Supreme Court judge, we'd be lost and defenseless in our guilt. Thankfully, Christ is our completely capable lawyer and the case *for* us rests *with* him and his atoning death for us.

That death is here depicted in the bread and cup which we now take.

Softness and Severity
Scripture: Romans 11:22

▼ ▼ ▼ ▼ ▼ ▼ ▼ ▼ ▼ ▼ ▼ ▼ ▼ ▼ ▼ ▼ ▼ ▼

INTERACTIVE IDEA

Ask members of your congregation to form groups of three or four, and ask at least two people within each group to share a time they remember when a parent or other adult was too *soft* on them. Ask them to briefly discuss why they felt that way, and what the consequences were.

WHAT TO SAY

In Romans 11:22 Paul zeroes in on two sides of our omni-sided God—his *softness* and his *severity*. While we often regard these qualities as mutually exclusive, they're similar to the characteristics we talk about when we say, "Love the sinner while hating the sin."

Every Old Testament priest had to be a master model of these two attributes. He had to be sensitive toward the sinner, for he was a sin-consultant. His job profile demanded that he not turn sinners away, for they were exactly the people he was there to help (Hebrews 5:1-2). But at the same time, no priest could afford to be lax (as Eli was toward his sons' sins in 1 Samuel 2) when it came to dealing with people's sins.

In Christ's cross, the concepts of mercy and justice kissed each other. Miraculously, the divine judge is also the pardoner. God's demand for justice is satisfied through Christ's assumption of our injustices. Because his justice has been satisfied, his mercy flows freely to all who are open to receive it.

In communion, we are drinking in the chemistry of his justice and mercy, his softness and sternness. Partake. It's for you.

Unfathomable Depths
Scripture: Romans 11:33

▼ ▼ ▼ ▼ ▼ ▼ ▼ ▼ ▼ ▼ ▼ ▼ ▼ ▼ ▼ ▼ ▼ ▼

BACKGROUND

Anyone who's had an exploratory look at coral formations and underwater plant life can only marvel at the exotic world beneath the surface of the sea.

WHAT TO SAY

In Romans 11:33, Paul exclaims, "Oh, the depth of the riches of the wisdom and knowledge of God. How unsearchable his judgments!"

Maybe you've been to one of those big aquariums where you actually walk next to sea life. Or maybe you've been scuba diving. Imagine getting an even closer and more in-depth look at an underwater world. Maybe this is why Paul chose the metaphor of underwater "depths" to capture something of the marvel and mystery of all God is and all he has done for us.

Inside of every human are hidden depths of secret sin and shame. Every time some stalker-murderer is revealed by newspaper headlines, people are shocked at the sin that was hiding beneath the surface. Yet how many of us would want our sins to be suddenly flashed on a public screen? Thankfully, believers know that God "will...hurl all our iniquities [or sins] into the depths of the sea" (Micah 7:19).

What awesome depths this bread and this cup represent—that all our secret sin and shame are covered in the depths of God's unfathomable love. Reflect on that today as you enter into communion.

Chapter 6

The Early Church:
Meditations From the Epistles

The Three E's

Celestial Mathematics

Gratis and Gratitude

The Sacrificial Buck Jones

The I's Have It

Stupendous Salvation

Divine Dimensions

Take Two Giant Steps

In Civvies

What's "Therefore" There For?

What's in a Name?

Here's Richness

Cosmic Conundrum

X Marks the Spot

Incomparable Treasure

Calvary as Auschwitz

Old Faithful

An Enjoyable Deity

Unstuck From a Cradle or Cross!

Re-Circuited Relationships

A Thousand Sacred Sweets

Uncollared Priests

D-Day Invasion

The Three E's
Scripture: 1 Corinthians 15:3-4

▼ ▼ ▼ ▼ ▼ ▼ ▼ ▼ ▼ ▼ ▼ ▼ ▼ ▼ ▼ ▼ ▼ ▼ ▼

BACKGROUND

Thousands of citizens in the Roman Empire were crucified, yet only one "died for our sins." Travelers passed by that crucifixion scene, yet only an enlightened few knew the explanation of that middle-cross crucifixion. All others died; Christ died *for our sins.*

WHAT TO SAY

I'd like to talk for just a minute about three E's from 1 Corinthians 15:3-4—event, evidence, and explanation. These verses supply the very foundation of the gospel.

Event A—Christ died.

Explanation A—for our sins

Evidence A—He was buried.

Event B—He was raised.

Evidence B—He appeared.

[It may be helpful to print these statements on a chalkboard or project them on a screen in front of your congregation.]

The evidence is rock-solid. Crucified corpses don't survive three-day interments. Furthermore, his resurrection is eyewitness-real, for he was seen by more than a thousand eyes (1 Corinthians 15:6).

Now, I—and you—must transfer this empirical evidence to the realm of experience. I must apply the meaning to myself: "He died for *my* sins." When I realize and accept that reality, I find forgiveness full and free.

Someone present today may have never experienced the reality of the full and free forgiveness Christ offers. If you by faith receive Christ for yourself, then you're welcome to join with us in your first Christian communion. Then, as you take the bread and the cup, you're acknowledging with the rest of us that Christ died for *our* sins.

INTERACTIVE IDEA

Ask members of the congregation to turn to another person and say, "I believe in the forgiveness of sins through personal faith in Jesus Christ." Or read the "Event, Evidence, Explanation" list above as a responsive or unison reading.

Celestial Mathematics
Scripture: 2 Corinthians 5:21;
Hebrews 10:17

▼ ▼ ▼ ▼ ▼ ▼ ▼ ▼ ▼ ▼ ▼ ▼ ▼ ▼ ▼ ▼ ▼ ▼

USE THE UNUSUAL

Place on your platform an old chalkboard covered with an imaginary, unsolvable math problem.

WHAT TO SAY

In elementary school most of us learn to grasp basic math. Subtraction and addition are almost fun. But as we progress through school, tackling geometry, algebra, and calculus, the math problems become increasingly difficult.

When we personally accept Christ as Savior, the most titanic *subtraction* and *addition* take place. All sins are *subtracted*; eternal life is *added* to the account of the new Christian. God even forgets our sins (Hebrews 8:12; 10:17) because they have been subtracted.

Oddly, this subtraction occurs by means of a *plus sign*. The standard cross is simply a lengthened extension of a plus sign. God's plus sign—the cross—affirms the positive subtraction of our sins.

Beyond this *subtraction* is the *addition* of Christ's imputed righteousness to believers (Romans 4:6; 2 Corinthians 5:21). We become

"Dressed in His righteousness alone,

Faultless to stand before [God's] throne."

—Edward Mote

God's math doesn't stop there. Once we've experienced God's subtraction and addition, out of gratitude we should seek the *multiplication* of Christian virtues (2 Peter 1:5-7) in our lives.

Today, as we approach this communion gathering, let's ask God to inspire us to cultivate Christian character. Christ voluntarily sacrificed himself in death, which is what communion is all about. Therefore, we seek to be in communion with him so that his character be reflected in our lives.

We now partake of communion because Christ took our sins on himself—and they are *subtracted* forever! Carry this aspect of communion with you as you go forth from this table into the larger world around you.

Gratis and Gratitude
Scripture: 2 Corinthians 8:9; 9:15

▼ ▼ ▼ ▼ ▼ ▼ ▼ ▼ ▼ ▼ ▼ ▼ ▼ ▼ ▼ ▼ ▼

INTERACTIVE IDEA

Ask those participating in the service to cluster in trios and share one thing they're thankful for because of God's great grace.

WHAT TO SAY

Gratis and gratitude. Let's talk for a minute about these two G words.

It doesn't take a great detective to figure out that these two words are related linguistically. They're related as cause and effect. In fact, the very same exquisite Greek word in the New Testament, *charis* [KARR-iss], is translated as both "grace" and "thanks" in different contexts.

In 2 Corinthians 8:9, we read of the grace *(charis)* of our Lord Jesus in his stoop to humanity and death. Yet one chapter later (in 2 Corinthians 9:15) the very same Greek word *(charis)* is translated as "thanks"—"Thanks be to God for his indescribable gift!"

Grace begets gratitude. *Gratitude* is the proper response to what God has done *gratis* for us. Only the *ungrateful* will take a gift and not say thank you.

Because Christ took the cross, we take the cup. Because he offered his body to be brutalized, we accept the bread from his gracious nail-scarred hand. We *gratefully* receive what he *graciously* gave.

The Sacrificial Buck Jones
Scripture: Galatians 1:4

▼ ▼ ▼ ▼ ▼ ▼ ▼ ▼ ▼ ▼ ▼ ▼ ▼ ▼ ▼ ▼ ▼ ▼

WHAT TO SAY

Kids in the early twentieth century grew up with movie cowboy heroes such as Tom Mix, Hoot Gibson, and Buck Jones.

Buck Jones' life ended inside a Boston club one evening when it caught fire. He could have escaped and spared his own life. But Jones played a real-life hero by going back into the burning building to rescue others. As a result, Jones died, giving his own life to save others.

Similarly, on September 11, 2001, many firefighters unselfishly gave their lives for others in the World Trade Center tragedy. Afterward, they were remembered at both local and national memorial services.

Galatians 1:4 indicates that the Lord Jesus Christ gave himself on our behalf. The Savior sacrificed himself for our sins. This is precisely what we commemorate in communion: "His body—for me; his blood—for me. I should have suffered what he suffered."

We remember him in his death as he requested. He sacrificed himself "to rescue us" (Galatians 1:4) from a fiery future. Take, eat, experience. Remember your remarkable rescuer.

USE THE UNUSUAL

Project a scene of the World Trade Towers on a screen to remind listeners of the rescue personnel who unselfishly gave their lives to save others.

The I's Have It
Scripture: Galatians 2:20
▼　▼　▼　▼　▼　▼　▼　▼　▼　▼　▼　▼　▼　▼　▼　▼　▼　▼

BACKGROUND

Galatians 2:20 is one of those wall-plaque verses. It says Christians have been crucified with Christ, yet still live. Furthermore, Christ lives inside of us, and we live by faith in God's Son who gave his life for us. While many Christians can quote this verse, how many really understand it?

INTERACTIVE IDEA

If you're comfortable using different Bible versions, ask people ahead of time to read Galatians 2:20 consecutively from as many translations and paraphrases as possible.

WHAT TO SAY

Galatians 2:20 is one of those verses that sounds confusing, but it's packed with wonderful meaning. From this verse, we observe

1. a new reality—I am co-crucified with Christ.
2. a new resident—Christ lives inside me.
3. a new reliance—"I live by faith."
4. a new relationship—he "loved me and gave himself for me."

If the verses were merely "me-istic," they'd instill a cult of self-centeredness. Yet each "I" in the verse places us individually within the orbit of Christ's personalized love. "Oh the wonder of such a thought—that he loves *me.*"

Because he loves millions of "me's," he politely requests all of us to remember him. He sought us, bought us, brought us, and taught us. Therefore, we remember his person and work. We commune with our living Lord, for we died with him, rose with him, and live with and for him. We have good reasons to remember him.

While Galatians 2:20 is filled with "I's," when we share the bread and cup, each "I" is individually important to God. We're not absorbed into some great invisible world-ocean. Rather, we understand as we partake of these elements that they stand for his personalized love for each one of us.

Stupendous Salvation
Scripture: Ephesians 2:8-10

▼ ▼ ▼ ▼ ▼ ▼ ▼ ▼ ▼ ▼ ▼ ▼ ▼ ▼ ▼ ▼ ▼ ▼

OBJECT LESSON

Hold up an old-fashioned pocket watch, and make note of the works inside—gears and inner works that enable it to keep time. In our age of advanced technology, a watch doesn't seem all that amazing, but consider that pocket watches have been around for hundreds of years.

BACKGROUND

For this meditation, be sure to read aloud Ephesians 2:8-10 before you move on to the "What to Say" section.

WHAT TO SAY

These verses carry the weighty and invaluable cargo of salvation. In this jewel case we find the *cause, channel,* and *consequence* of salvation.

- The *cause* of salvation is *grace*—God's sheer and undeserved generosity offered to undeserving and hell-deserving sinners. Only by grace does anyone stand saved.
- The *channel* of salvation is *faith.* Salvation comes by faith alone through grace alone in Christ alone. Works are excluded (Romans 3:28; 4:4-5; 11:6).
- The *consequence* of salvation is the Christian's good works. Every Christian should be like a fine Swiss watch—full of good works. Can you tutor a needy child, cut an elderly person's grass, help a single mother repair her car, take an immigrant through proper legal procedures, spend time with a next-door neighbor?

Though we don't work for salvation, we work *because of* salvation; we are God's workmanship (Ephesians 2:10).

One visible sign of our salvation is taking communion because Christ instructed us to do so. It's a simple good work that you can do today. Fortunately, some efforts are also extremely enjoyable. To know we're pleasing Christ as we carry out his instructions—this worthwhile work gives us pleasure as well!

USE THE UNUSUAL

Ask someone with a rather dramatic personal testimony to tell the events surrounding putting his or her personal trust in Christ.

Divine Dimensions
Scripture: Ephesians 3:18

▼ ▼ ▼ ▼ ▼ ▼ ▼ ▼ ▼ ▼ ▼ ▼ ▼ ▼ ▼ ▼ ▼ ▼

BACKGROUND

In Ephesians 3:18, Paul takes dimensional soundings as to "how wide and long and high and deep is the love of Christ." It's as if he's a submarine captain heading down, down, down. Yet one dimension is insufficient to describe the vastness of God's inimitable love. So Paul pictures four dimensions.

INTERACTIVE IDEA

Before the service, select photos that represent the dimensions of height, depth, length, and width. Pass these photos down the aisles of worshippers. If you have time, ask one person from each row to comment on the pictures. (For example, someone might say, "This skyscraper reminds me of looking out over the harbor in New York City from atop the Statue of Liberty.")

WHAT TO SAY

We might as well try to measure the ocean in a thimble as figure out the dimensions of God's love. As one song, "O the Deep, Deep Love of Jesus" by Samuel Trevor Francis, expresses it, the love of Jesus is "vast, unmeasured, boundless, free! Rolling as a mighty ocean in its fullness over me."

The corresponding human reflex to God's oceanic love should be found in our devoted response. We measure out the liquid and pour it into a cup and drink that small measure at communion. That represents the size of our love compared to his—and even then we are taking and he is giving. What an awesome God we serve!

Take Two Giant Steps
Scripture: Philippians 2:5-8

▼ ▼ ▼ ▼ ▼ ▼ ▼ ▼ ▼ ▼ ▼ ▼ ▼ ▼ ▼ ▼ ▼ ▼

WHAT TO SAY

Did you ever play that childhood game—some people called it "Master, May I...?"—where the caller invites you to take "six baby steps" or "three scissor steps" or "two giant steps" and so on? In the game, if you forget to ask permission, you're forced to return to the starting line.

In Philippians 2:5-8, the Lord of glory took *two giant* steps. Step one was the incarnation; step two was his crucifixion.

In the first giant step, he "made himself nothing" (Philippians 2:7). While he didn't surrender his deity, he "made himself nothing" by setting aside his glory and submitting to the humiliation of becoming human.

In the second giant step, "he humbled himself" (Philippians 2:8). Having become *human,* he endured the *inhumane*—even the future torture of the cross. His death on the cross, which is the word *crux* in Latin, was excruciating. Even in the very pronunciation of the word *excruciating,* we hear the extreme awfulness of a crux or cross.

Christ took two giant steps—when he remembered us—in the incarnation as a servant and in the degrading act of crucifixion. In Christ, God stooped to the level of a slave. He came down to lift us up. Someday we'll enter heaven because he took our hell.

We take but a small step when we remember him in his death by means of the two communion elements. As we do this simple thing he has asked us to do, allow the act to draw out your devotion to the God of the giant steps.

OBJECT LESSON

If you can procure any samples of crosses (whether ornate, rough, or famous paintings), hold them up and talk briefly about the horrible death endured by people who were crucified.

In Civvies
Scripture: Philippians 2:7

▼ ▼ ▼ ▼ ▼ ▼ ▼ ▼ ▼ ▼ ▼ ▼ ▼ ▼ ▼ ▼ ▼ ▼

OBJECT LESSON

Display some type of military memorabilia, such as chevrons or medals.

INTERACTIVE IDEA

Ask worshippers to share with one person nearby how someone "pulled rank" on them. (Caution them not to divulge identities or mention people who are present.)

WHAT TO SAY

[Read Philippians 2:7 aloud.] **The great scholar Bishop Lightfoot of Durham, England, paraphrased this classic text by saying, "He stripped himself of the insignia of majesty." Dr. Merrill Tenney of Wheaton College amplified the paraphrase into an illustration.**

Suppose, noted Tenney, that a ranking officer enters a military barracks in full-dress uniform. All the enlisted soldiers there instantly snap to attention. They respect his rank. However, suppose that just a few minutes later, the very same person enters the barracks—only this time without the uniform. In effect, he has stripped off his stripes. No longer do the enlistees snap to salute, because (in Lightfoot's majestic terms) he has "stripped himself of the insignia of majesty."

God's Son arrived on our planet in "civvies," so to speak, without any of the glory or splendor that was due to him as King of kings and Lord of lords. He did not display his Godness in eye-blinding magnificence. Instead, he looked like us. He "surrendered his stripes." His body looked ordinary.

The bread and cup before us look ordinary—yet they represent the reality of God entering ordinary humanity to do the extraordinary for us. As you partake of these very common elements, ponder the extraordinary work Christ did in his human form.

What's "Therefore" There For?
Scripture: Philippians 2:9

▼ ▼ ▼ ▼ ▼ ▼ ▼ ▼ ▼ ▼ ▼ ▼ ▼ ▼ ▼ ▼ ▼

WHAT TO SAY

A male of college age once remarked to a female student, "I was sick after I last saw you." She laughed, because it sounded like the male had gotten sick *because* he'd seen her recently. She made the mistake of equating a *subsequent* event with a *consequent* event. Subsequence merely implies a before-and-after sequence, whereas consequence indicates a cause-and-effect sequence.

The Bible often makes use of the word *therefore* when a clear-cut cause-and-effect transition is taking place. We should always ask, "What is 'therefore' there for?"

In Philippians 2:9, the "therefore" is a gate hinge swinging back to what's just come before. It announces: "Therefore God [the Father] exalted [Christ] to the highest place." Because of Christ's humiliation (Philippians 2:6-8), God the Father bestowed on him the appropriate exalted level. The "therefore" in 2:9 is a conclusion which comes as a consequence and not from mere before-and-after sequence.

Because Christ stooped to the cross of shame, we bow before his well-deserved fame. We commune with the crown head of the cosmos! In communion, we can visualize with the bread and the cup just how low he stooped for us.

OBJECT LESSON

Display a crown or valuable jewels to help communicate the majesty of His Majesty, our Lord.

What's in a Name?
Scripture: Philippians 2:10

INTERACTIVE IDEA

Ask some of the children from your church to tell what name or nickname they'd give themselves if they had a choice. Keep in mind that children often want to be funny, so decide ahead of time if your congregation will be comfortable with a lighter moment right before communion.

WHAT TO SAY

Charles the Bold, Leif the Lucky, Artaxerxes the Long-Handed, Alexander the Great—such are the epithets attached to some of history's most heralded humans.

What a contrast to what we read in Philippians 2:10 "that at the [simple] name of Jesus every knee should bow."

While we call him Christ, Messiah, Lord, God, Master, Teacher, Redeemer, Savior, and a whole parade of other titles, we relish the simply sublime name of Jesus. As the praise song of a few decades ago says, "There's just something about that name." His is the name above all names.

Not only does Christ *deserve* the name above all names, but he supplies new names to us even though we *don't* deserve them. To his followers, Jesus will one day give a "stone with a new name written on it, known only to him [or her] who receives it" (Revelation 2:17). We'll receive a special name from the one who has the superlative name.

He "calls his own sheep by name" (John 10:3). Imagine him calling you into communion with him. "John, Bill, Harry, Mary, LeShawn, Theresa [or substitute names of people in your congregation]," he says, "Take this bread; this is my body given for you. Take this cup; it's my blood shed for you."

He calls each of you by name. Imagine that!

Here's Richness
Scripture: Philippians 4:19

▼ ▼ ▼ ▼ ▼ ▼ ▼ ▼ ▼ ▼ ▼ ▼ ▼ ▼ ▼ ▼ ▼ ▼

OBJECT LESSON

Hold up objects that will help people think of wealth. For example, brightly polished, multicolored rocks from a gift store might make young children's eyes sparkle. For adults, display an impressive-looking deed, a document signifying stock ownership, or fine jewelry.

BACKGROUND

All earth's treasures pale compared to the "glorious riches in Christ Jesus."

WHAT TO SAY

Charles Dickens' villains are frequently *comic* villains. If they were mere villains, no one would laugh at them. But Dickens introduces us to the villainous dwarf, Daniel Quilp, in *The Old Curiosity Shop*. Quilp gulps his boiling tea straight down without a wink and eats his boiled eggs, eggshells and all.

Dickens depicted another comic villain in *Nicholas Nickleby*—the cruel schoolmaster, Mr. Squeers. At one point, Squeers heavily dilutes a boy's glass of milk with water and announces to the aghast boy, "Here's richness!"

When we consider the content of our communion, we can truthfully say, "Here's richness!" For us there are "rivers flowing with honey and cream" (Job 20:17). God "satisfies you with the finest of wheat" (Psalm 147:14). "Your soul will delight in the richest of fare" (Isaiah 55:2). While we may feel we are poor, we have the key to God's "glorious riches in Christ Jesus" (Philippians 4:19).

Of course, you wouldn't have to be rich to purchase the items used here today on this tray and in this cup. Yet these elements were purchased with the immeasurable sacrifice of God himself. Therefore, as we partake of these elements, we can truly say, "Here's richness!"

Cosmic Conundrum
Scripture: Colossians 1:17

▼ ▼ ▼ ▼ ▼ ▼ ▼ ▼ ▼ ▼ ▼ ▼ ▼ ▼ ▼ ▼ ▼ ▼

WHAT TO SAY

Colossians 1:17 portrays Christ as God's glue—the cosmic cement that holds the whole world together. What secular scientists label *gravity*, Christians call *Christ*.

John 1:3 and Hebrews 1:2 reinforce the truth of Colossians 1:17. Christ is co-creator of the universe. No wonder he could walk on this world's water or instantly change water to wine!

How could a baby simultaneously be God? The biblical data announce that "in Christ all the fullness of the Deity lives in bodily form" (Colossians 2:9). Fabulous, yet factual. Baffling, yet biblical. Astounding, yet actual.

The God who encapsulated himself in a body now expresses himself to us in bread. The very human blood that flowed through his veins and pumped through his heart, he now expresses in the liquid in this cup. He became a material flesh-form so that we can partake mystically and figuratively of the body and blood he gave for us.

Ponder. Wonder. Contemplate "the wonder of it all."

X Marks the Spot
Scripture: Colossians 2:3

▼ ▼ ▼ ▼ ▼ ▼ ▼ ▼ ▼ ▼ ▼ ▼ ▼ ▼ ▼ ▼ ▼ ▼

USE THE UNUSUAL

Ask someone to read from Robert Louis Stevenson's *Treasure Island* the section early in the story in which Jim Hawkins discovers the treasure map in Cap'n Billy Bones' sea chest. Note to your congregation that when we think of treasure maps we've seen in movies or even animated cartoons, we think of an X marking the spot of the treasure.

WHAT TO SAY

Today I want to ramble a bit about the symbol X, and share some things about Christ that we can remember with this simple symbol.

Virtually everyone in the Western world recognizes the traditional form of the cross that Christ reputedly died upon. However, the St. Andrew's cross-form is X-shaped, and it may have been used in ancient times as well. The Bible doesn't state the specific form that Christ's cross took. Could it have been an X?

The *X-Files* was a popular television program about solving bizarre mysteries. It is quite a mystery why God puts up with our repeated sins. Each of us has our own X-files cabinet.

On a treasure map X often designates the spot where riches are hidden. Our treasures are in Christ (Colossians 2:3). And we treasure those moments when we concentrate upon the gold bullion that we have in him.

Our time of communion highlights these treasured moments when we experience and enjoy the riches of Christ's wealth and worth.

Incomparable Treasure
Scripture: Colossians 2:3

▼ ▼ ▼ ▼ ▼ ▼ ▼ ▼ ▼ ▼ ▼ ▼ ▼ ▼ ▼ ▼ ▼ ▼

BACKGROUND

Just as you can find in the word *treasures* all the various nuances of any given word, so in *Christ* are many exquisite shades of meaning. This meditation looks at the Greek term for *treasures* in Colossians 2:3; in Greek, it's pronounced *thay-sah-ROY*. From it we get the English word *thesaurus*.

OBJECT LESSON

Hold up a copy of a thesaurus, explaining that it is a dictionary of synonyms.

WHAT TO SAY

A ship's shape appears silhouetted against the horizon. But the peaceful image is shattered. A small village on the shore is wracked with terror because the flag flying from the ship boasts a skull and crossbones. It's a pirate ship.

The folks aboard the "good ship Colosse" were threatened by philosophical pirates. Paul warned his Colossian readers that such people might take them captive (Colossians 2:8). You can pretty much count on pirates to hang around wherever there are treasures to be had. In Christ, Paul penned, are "hidden all the treasures of wisdom and knowledge" (Colossians 2:3).

Our treasure in Christ is "precious" (1 Peter 2:7), "immeasurably more than all we...imagine" (Ephesians 3:20). We have "incomparable riches" (Ephesians 2:7), "unsearchable riches" (Ephesians 3:8), and "glorious riches" (Ephesians 3:16; Philippians 4:19). Paul could refer to himself as "poor, yet making many rich" (2 Corinthians 6:10).

We experience the inestimable treasure trove of God's love. Are we relishing today the "riches of God's grace that he lavished on us" (Ephesians 1:7-8)? A bite of this bread—to the truly attuned—is better than a bite of a chocolate éclair. A sip of this cup—for the discerning—is richer than a drink of the most prized vintage wine.

Do you treasure these elements as you take them? The bread is broadcasting, Christ's riches were sacrificed for you. The cup is communicating, Christ's precious blood was given for you. Think of them as receipts for the riches that are yours in Christ.

Calvary as Auschwitz
Scripture: 2 Thessalonians 1:8-10

▼ ▼ ▼ ▼ ▼ ▼ ▼ ▼ ▼ ▼ ▼ ▼ ▼ ▼ ▼ ▼ ▼ ▼

INTERACTIVE IDEA

Invite people to turn to one other person and share the scenes that pop into their minds when they hear the word *horror.*

WHAT TO SAY

I can't imagine anything more horrific than the events that transpired in Nazi death camps such as Auschwitz, Belzen, and Treblinka. Jewish individuals, indeed human history, won't (and shouldn't) get over those horrors.

Yet I wonder how many people have ever thought of Calvary as a miniature version of Auschwitz. Like Auschwitz, Calvary was a kind of human holocaust, the cross a fiendish torture rack. In fact, the Greek word from which *holocaust* is derived pertains to the Old Testament burnt offering where the entire animal sacrifice was consumed by fire.

Jesus endured his personal Auschwitz precisely so that all people everywhere might avoid an eternal Auschwitz. [At this point, read aloud 2 Thessalonians 1:8-10.]

Jesus underwent the grim gore of Golgotha for our eternal comfort. He took our hell.

In communion, he offers us heavenly tokens. "I bore your hell; I offer you my heaven," he says. "Don't settle for an eternal Auschwitz when you can experience the fullness of eternal life."

Old Faithful
Scripture: 1 Timothy 6:15-16

▼ ▼ ▼ ▼ ▼ ▼ ▼ ▼ ▼ ▼ ▼ ▼ ▼ ▼ ▼ ▼ ▼

WHAT TO SAY

Old Faithful, the famous geyser in Yellowstone National Park, can be counted on to erupt at regular intervals. Similarly, Paul offers up praise-geysers at almost regular intervals, particularly in the books of Timothy and Titus.

First Timothy 6:15-16 offers us a sampling of one of these brilliant praise-geysers. Nestled in this text is a cluster of the attributes of God. God is

- blessed,
- monotheistic ("only"),
- sovereign ("ruler"),
- immortal (undying),
- unapproachable (except through Christ),
- invisible, and
- honorable.

As Walters Chalmers Smith put it:

"Immortal, invisible, God only wise,

In light inaccessible hid from our eyes."

Think of it! Our God, who resides in scorching, radiating, splendid light, unapproachable, approaches us in human form. In the bread of communion, we revel in this revelation—that God has lowered himself to come among us, to come as one of us, and to die for us. Charles Wesley asked:

"Amazing love! How can it be,

That Thou, my God, shouldst die for me?"

Paul's writings erupted with praise geysers. What praise can you silently offer to God today for what he's done for you?

USE THE UNUSUAL

Project a photo or find a video of Old Faithful or another geyser erupting. Your local library may have an educational video about geysers.

An Enjoyable Deity
Scripture: 1 Timothy 6:17

▼ ▼ ▼ ▼ ▼ ▼ ▼ ▼ ▼ ▼ ▼ ▼ ▼ ▼ ▼ ▼ ▼

INTERACTIVE IDEA

Ask people to gather in groups of four or five. Have each person suggest one thing that he or she truly *enjoys* (such as chocolate ice cream, skiing in Colorado, lying on a beach). After a few minutes, comment, "I wonder how often we associate the word *enjoy* with God."

WHAT TO SAY

If you search any standard tome on systematic theology, it's unlikely that you'll find this word listed under the attributes of God: enjoyability. Yet the classic Westminster Confession of Faith urges its constituents "to enjoy [God] forever." First Timothy 6:17 says that God "provides us with everything for our enjoyment." How strange it would be if the God who provides us "with everything for our enjoyment" couldn't be enjoyed!

Perhaps some sour-minded, lemon-lipped Christians get their image of God largely from Matthew 25:24, when the unfaithful steward pictured God under the image of "a hard man." Certainly if you think of God as austere and awful, you're hardly likely to enjoy such a deity!

Is your God *enjoyable*? If you're not entirely comfortable with the idea of an enjoyable God, it's probably time for a revised version of him. And if this enjoyable God gives us "everything for our enjoyment," then he strongly desires to meet with us in communion.

Have you ever seen a flock of birds taking off together and experienced some of God's beauty, just enjoying what God has put here in our world? Do you ever tax your brain to come up with a fresh attribute of God so as to enjoy him even more? Do you create any metaphors about God while celebrating communion?

Take. Partake. And, as waiters say, "Enjoy!"

Unstuck From a Cradle or Cross!
Scripture: 2 Timothy 2:8

▼ ▼ ▼ ▼ ▼ ▼ ▼ ▼ ▼ ▼ ▼ ▼ ▼ ▼ ▼ ▼ ▼ ▼

OBJECT LESSON

Display a typical crèche or manger scene found at Christmastime.

WHAT TO SAY

If you woke from a deep sleep suddenly and your mind flitted to Christ, how would you picture him? As a figure in a department store Nativity scene? Forever frozen as a baby in a manger? Forever affixed to the cross?

Do you ever imagine him as Paul urged in 2 Timothy 2:8: "Remember Jesus Christ as having been raised from the dead!" This is how that verse might be translated.

When we celebrate communion, we do as he asked. We remember him. But *how* do we remember him?

Remembering Jesus Christ in his death (as we do in communion) isn't the same as remembering Jesus Christ *as dead*. One hymn depicts the once-dead, now-living Lord:

> "By faith I look where Christ has gone,
> And see upon His Father's throne
> A Man, with glory crowned...
> In every wound I read my guilt,
> And thank Him that His blood was spilt."
> —C.E. Peglar

We can remember him in his death (as we do in communion), but it's not intended to be some morose memory. We can remember him as he now is—risen, crowned, glorious, and glorified until he comes again (1 Corinthians 11:26).

What emotions does this picture of the risen Christ evoke within you? It's hard to feel gloomy when you're imagining the living Lord. As you celebrate communion today, try to identify your emotions as you think of the One who died as one who is risen from the dead.

Re-Circuited Relationships
Scripture: Philemon 15-16

▼　▼　▼　▼　▼　▼　▼　▼　▼　▼　▼　▼　▼　▼　▼　▼　▼　▼

BACKGROUND

Imagine an old Victorian house that needs to be refurbished. Imagine that it needs total rewiring. Something comparable to that re-circuitry process happened when Christ came.

USE THE UNUSUAL

Precede your meditation by having two individuals approach each other, one from each side of the platform. One is dressed, as we say, "to kill," wearing a formal gown and jewelry or a tuxedo. The other person is dressed as a tattered homeless person. Yet the two mime a conversation as if on equal terms. They freeze at your signal while you move forward into the meditation.

WHAT TO SAY

One Christmas song, "O Holy Night," proclaims that "the slave is our brother." While we rarely see garbage collectors eating lunch with bank vice presidents, Christ's invasion of our planet began with a bulldozing process in the social sphere.

Paul announced to a patrician who easily could have been a big plantation owner that a human thing (or slave) should be treated "no longer as a slave, but...as a dear brother" (Philemon 16). What an ego-flattener! In effect, Paul handed his credit card to Philemon and said, "I'll pick up any tab Onesimus may have run up. I'll pay his bill."

Now imagine Philemon the plantation owner and Onesimus the slave sitting down side by side at a communion celebration. God's bulldozer has brought a change about in both their social and spiritual status.

In truest communion God brings together a kaleidoscope of people. Imagine yourself in the vastly larger world of God's people right now. Every color of skin, every nuance of culture, every level of education, every strata of society is represented.

As you take communion today, thank God that he so loved the world— and not just a select segment of society.

A Thousand Sacred Sweets
Scripture: 1 Peter 1:8

▼ ▼ ▼ ▼ ▼ ▼ ▼ ▼ ▼ ▼ ▼ ▼ ▼ ▼ ▼ ▼ ▼ ▼

USE THE UNUSUAL

Before the service, ask a soloist to learn the music to the chorus noted in the first paragraph below, and ask that person to sing it. As the soloist sings, hold up a series of candy bars and other sweets.

WHAT TO SAY

In his hymn "Come We That Love the Lord," hymn writer Isaac Watts informed us that "the hill of Zion yields a thousand sacred sweets." It sounds much like a Candyland or a child's version of heaven. C.S. Lewis, a famous British scholar, talked about a longing for something indefinably sweet.

Those who've enjoyed the richness of deep communion with Christ can genuinely imagine "a thousand sacred sweets." Though we partake of simple bread and drink from a simple cup, as C. Austin Miles wrote, "Joy we share as we tarry there, none other has ever known." We're insiders—in on a secret sweetness that others can't even imagine. Peter said that though we haven't seen him, we're "filled with an inexpressible and glorious joy" (1 Peter 1:8). Inexpressibly sweet! For some of us, communion is a confectioner's shop.

Think in those terms as the bread and cup are received today. What is inexpressibly sweet to you about Christ and his cross? As you partake, let your mind focus on the joy and sweetness of a thousand sacred sweets.

Uncollared Priests
Scripture: 1 Peter 2:5, 9

▼ ▼ ▼ ▼ ▼ ▼ ▼ ▼ ▼ ▼ ▼ ▼ ▼ ▼ ▼ ▼ ▼ ▼

BACKGROUND

In spite of some negative actions of priests in the Roman Catholic church, we shouldn't let this very small contingent of people change the way Scripture defines the true priesthood.

WHAT TO SAY

All God's people are a "kingdom of priests" (Exodus 19:6). **And we're not to be mute priests, because we're appointed to advertise our Lord's excellencies** (1 Peter 2:9).

You might also say that we're a knightly priesthood. Knighthood conjures up beautifully colored banners, snorting stallions, jousting tournaments, and shiny armor. The idea of Old Testament priesthood conjures up images of white turbans, gold-plated headbands, multicolored uniforms, and the smell of roasting lamb.

Here we are—a priesthood of Christ's knights around his round table, partaking and participating as priests. Priest Martha, Priest Jerry, Priest George, and so forth. Priests, let us eat and drink as a royal priesthood!

We don't wear the armor of knights or priestly vestments, yet we're a holy and royal priesthood (1 Peter 2:5, 9). **So we partake of priest fare in the form of this bread and cup. Let these images wash over you as you enjoy communion today.**

D-Day Invasion
Scripture: 1 John 4:2

▼ ▼ ▼ ▼ ▼ ▼ ▼ ▼ ▼ ▼ ▼ ▼ ▼ ▼ ▼ ▼ ▼ ▼

INTERACTIVE IDEA

Ask each member of your congregation to share with someone nearby how some other Christian demonstrated Christ's love for him or her in a memorable way.

WHAT TO SAY

On June 6, 1944, the Allies—at great cost of life—undertook the D-Day invasion by staking out a beachhead on the coast of Normandy.

First John 4:2 describes the truth of a still-greater invasion. God invaded planet Earth in the incarnation. "Jesus Christ has come in the flesh." That is, God the Son became a human being. Bethlehem was his beachhead.

Imagine all the private planning that went into the Normandy invasion. Consider the *prevision* that created God's *provision* for us. F.W. Boreham (in *My Christmas Book*) wrote: "Wren expressed himself in granite; Turner expressed himself in oils; Michelangelo expressed himself in marble; Shakespeare expressed himself in ink; but God selected *flesh* as the ideal vehicle for self-expression."

In Christ, God became one of us. It was the only way Christ could fully express his love, for his death required a human body.

G.K. Chesterton called the Incarnation "that incredible interruption, as a blow that broke the very backbone of history." This means that God invaded human history in a far greater way than the Allied invasion in 1944. History would never be the same.

God presented himself in a body, with flesh and blood. Now he presents himself in two simple elements—the bread and the cup. As we partake of them today, we acknowledge God's wonderful and necessary invasion of our world.

Chapter 7

The High Priest:
Meditations From Hebrews

The All-Superior Son

The Herculean Task

The Singing Savior

Centered

Anchored

Here It Is!

The World's Greatest Walkathon

The Amnesiac God

The All-Superior Son
Scripture: Hebrews 1–2

▼ ▼ ▼ ▼ ▼ ▼ ▼ ▼ ▼ ▼ ▼ ▼ ▼ ▼ ▼ ▼ ▼ ▼

INTERACTIVE IDEA

Ask members of your congregation to tell someone seated nearby about a person who they consider absolutely unique.

WHAT TO SAY

As the French might say, Jesus is *non-pareil* [nahn-puh-REHL]. He's unparalleled. He's one "without equal." He is the un-Xerox-able person of the universe. Hebrews 1:1–3:6 makes this claim clear. Let's look at a few examples.

God spoke through the prophets in the *past* days, but God has spoken in and through his own Son in these *last* days (Hebrews 1:1-3). He is *the* prophet without parallel (John 6:14). God hasn't left us on a silent planet but talks to us pre-eminently through Christ.

God's *Son* alone is superior to all the *sons* of God or angels (Job 38:6-7). No angel or human deserves worship (Hebrews 1:6; Acts 10:25-26; and Revelation 19:10); Christ alone is the object of our adoration.

Communion is a *locus*—or place—of worship when we *focus* in on his "worthship"—when we make Christ the one worthy of our worship. Why worship unless someone is significantly greater than we are—or worthy of our *wor*ship? Human beings instinctively react to something or someone greater than themselves—with quietness, reverence, or worship. That's exactly the reaction Jesus' disciples had to a human being who could calm a stormy sea in a single moment (Mark 4:39-41).

Communion is one form of worship. It is a reasonable and responsible response to the greatness of what Christ has done for each of us. He took our sins; we take the bread and cup. He redeemed us; we reverently recognize it and remember him by this appointed means of communing with him.

The Herculean Task
Scripture: Hebrews 1:3

▼　▼　▼　▼　▼　▼　▼　▼　▼　▼　▼　▼　▼　▼　▼　▼　▼　▼

USE THE UNUSUAL

Before the service, you might have an artist from your congregation draw the mythical figure Hercules engaging in some feat of strength. Or if your congregation is open to video usage, a clip from a Hercules movie might be briefly shown here.

WHAT TO SAY

In ancient Greek mythology, the king of Elis was named Augeas. Augeas was famed for his three thousand oxen, including twelve white bulls. One can imagine what a stable full of these oxen would produce if adequate stable hands failed to do their job properly.

One of the twelve tasks assigned to the legendary character Hercules was to clean Augeas' stables. In mythical fashion Hercules accomplished this task by rerouting the rivers of Alpheus and Peneius.

The purification of human pollution was the herculean task of the Son of God who "provided purification for [our] sins" (Hebrews 1:3). The Greek term for this feat in Hebrews 1:3 is related to the English word *catharsis*. A catharsis is a cleansing of emotions. Christ is our cleanser.

Even as we partake at the Lord's table, we confess our known sins (1 John 1:9) so that we may partake in a manner worthy of his cleansing work (1 Corinthians 11:27).

The Singing Savior
Scripture: Hebrews 2:12

▼ ▼ ▼ ▼ ▼ ▼ ▼ ▼ ▼ ▼ ▼ ▼ ▼ ▼ ▼ ▼ ▼ ▼

USE THE UNUSUAL

Ask a soloist to meld a series of communion hymns into a medley using one stanza from each hymn. Ask the congregation to join in singing a special communion hymn.

WHAT TO SAY

Do you remember the two occasions in the New Testament in which Jesus is said to sing? The first is the more obvious—at the Last Passover and first Christian communion (in Mark 14:26). (We presume he was included when "they" sang a hymn and exited from the upper room en route to the Mount of Olives.)

The second instance is less known. Hebrews 2:12 is derived from a Messianic psalm. Messianic psalms are those that contain clear-cut foreshadowing of Jesus the Messiah centuries before his birth. Psalm 22:22 (as quoted in Hebrews 2:12) says, "In the presence of the congregation I will sing your praises." The "I" here is the future Messiah speaking. This coming champion announces, "I will sing."

Zephaniah 3:17 says, "The Lord your God...will rejoice over you with singing." Here *even God* is said to sing. Thus, our *singing God!*

Remembering Hebrews 2:12, can we not imagine Christ as our musical maestro leading us in the future in celestial choruses—as both the subject and object of heaven's harmony?

So, even now as our singing reverberates here at communion, we expect to join in the heavenly choir of millions of Christ-worshippers around God's throne.

Our ears participate together in the sounds of heaven's praises, and our mouths participate in the remembrance of our Lord in his death until he comes again.

Centered
Scripture: Hebrews 4:14

▼ ▼ ▼ ▼ ▼ ▼ ▼ ▼ ▼ ▼ ▼ ▼ ▼ ▼ ▼ ▼ ▼ ▼

INTERACTIVE IDEA

What do you think of as being in the *center*? This might be a question you could let people discuss in pairs for a minute, as a lead-in to the meditation.

WHAT TO SAY

Practically in the center position in the book of Hebrews is the central idea of the book: We Christians have a great high priest in Jesus, the Son of God (Hebrews 4:14). The one on the middle cross at Calvary hit the problem head-on that was at the heart of humanity. The heart of the human problem is sin in the human heart. Therefore, our priest centered in on our most pervasive problem so that our hearts might be changed forever.

Christ came in order to come to terms with the central problem of our universe. Sin is at the center of all our most pervasive personal problems. Therefore, until a person lets Christ become central to his or her personality, he will always be on the periphery, on the outskirts of our lives.

Communion has a way of getting us back to what's central in God's concerns for us. What does your life revolve around? These two elements force us to hear Christ saying, "You are at the center of my concerns. Am I at the center of yours?" These outward things have a way of getting at the heart of things. So take these external elements and let them touch your internal self. He died for you.

Anchored
Scripture: Hebrews 6:19-20

▼ ▼ ▼ ▼ ▼ ▼ ▼ ▼ ▼ ▼ ▼ ▼ ▼ ▼ ▼ ▼ ▼ ▼

BACKGROUND

The author of Hebrews used an interesting metaphor. He envisioned an anchor for our souls with its chain stretching into the innermost cubicle or backroom of the heavenly tabernacle. The anchor portrays the solid prongs of Christian hope, which have their hold and home in heaven. This metaphor is found only here (Hebrews 6:19-20) in the New Testament.

USE THE UNUSUAL

Ask an artist to draw several coats of arms that you can briefly explain to lead into the meditation.

WHAT TO SAY

What does the picture of an anchor communicate to you? Holding power, being fixed or stationary, stability, sureness?

In the Roman catacombs, one early Christian named Priscilla had a tomb where archaeologists found a graphic representation of an anchor. For her—and for the author of Hebrews—the anchor is almost like a coat of arms.

Priscilla Owens later penned these words:

"We have an anchor that keeps the soul
Steadfast and sure while the billows roll."

Our faith has its anchor in real history. We're not a group of transcendental meditationists mystically fixated upon an ideal. Our Christ is as real as his glorified body. Our faith is as real as the tangible bread and cup. Our hope is not based on wishes. It's as hard and fast as an anchor.

In these two elements—the bread and cup—we have two tangible items. While they're not as hard and heavy as an anchor, they do tie us to the tangible world where we operate.

God gave us something tangible, visible, and edible to remind us of the invisible and eternal realities we Christians participate in. Eat the bread. Drink of the cup. Feel yourself anchored to the living Lord.

Here It Is!
Scripture: Hebrews 8:1

▼ ▼ ▼ ▼ ▼ ▼ ▼ ▼ ▼ ▼ ▼ ▼ ▼ ▼ ▼ ▼ ▼

BACKGROUND

On scenic Lookout Mountain near Chattanooga, Tennessee, some interesting signs dot the mountain highway. They read something like "See the man-eating python of the Jungle!" or "See the great Gila monster at the Jungle!" And, just in case you missed that fortress-like enclosure, you might meet a later sign inviting you to turn around and go back to the huge billboard reading "Here It Is: The Jungle!" Look out! At Lookout Mountain you'll see signs.

WHAT TO SAY

Hebrews 8:1 says, "The point of what we are saying is this: We do have such a high priest." In other words, "Here he is—just the high priest we've been needing all along!"

"It's a jungle out there," we say. And it's also a jungle in here [point inside yourself]. To penetrate any jungle, we need to use something as penetrating as a machete. Jesus makes a clearing in our inner jungle. He's the trailblazer who has gone where others cannot go.

Our trailblazer has now passed out of this earthly jungle and into heaven itself (Hebrews 4:14). Yet the one who has gone ahead of us to prepare a place for us has left us signs along the life-trail.

Two of these signs are in front of us this morning. One we eat and one we drink, yet they converge on the same reality. The bread ripped apart reminds us of Christ's body sacrificed for us. The cup of liquid makes us think of his lifeblood, which flowed out in death for us.

These two signs signal to us his undeniable love. Accept these two signs in loving remembrance of him.

The World's Greatest Walkathon
Scripture: Hebrews 9:6-9; 10:1-3, 11

▼ ▼ ▼ ▼ ▼ ▼ ▼ ▼ ▼ ▼ ▼ ▼ ▼ ▼ ▼ ▼ ▼ ▼

USE THE UNUSUAL

Arrange for children from your Sunday school classes to provide a parade of walkers who simply walk back and forth across the platform or up and down the aisles. Open by saying, "Ah. It looks like a *walkathon!*"

WHAT TO SAY

Tramp, tramp, tramp. Hear the sound of many footsteps. In and out. Back and forth. No rest for this group. They were in a walkathon—the world's greatest walkathon. They were Old Testament priests. They scurried back to sacrifice yet another sheep because someone else had sinned. An Old Testament priest's work was never done. Therefore, he walked and walked and walked some more.

If you were to walk into your favorite hamburger place and all the employees were sitting down, you might wonder, Are they on a break or on strike or is their work finished? People move around on their feet because their work is unfinished. They can sit when the work is done.

Yet when we walk through the door of the book of Hebrews, we see something unheard of in Old Testament history: a seated priest! After Christ offered himself as a sacrifice for sin, he "sat down" at the Father's right hand (Hebrews 1:3). This is why we can call the work of Christ on the cross finished! No more re-offering is required. His is the perfect and final sacrifice for sin.

That's why he is the seated priest. And we are seated at his table as we remember his finished work in absolving all our sins. Hallelujah! It is finished!

Today and each time we take the bread and cup, we simply remember what he's done. We don't need to worry about a to-do list of tasks to get God in our good graces. It's all grace. Receive his grace as you partake.

The Amnesiac God
Scripture: Hebrews 10:17

▼ ▼ ▼ ▼ ▼ ▼ ▼ ▼ ▼ ▼ ▼ ▼ ▼ ▼ ▼ ▼

INTERACTIVE IDEA

Invite individuals to trade stories about how they've forgotten something. After this time of sharing in pairs, begin by saying, "It might surprise you to realize that the all-knowing God is also the all-time champion forgetter!"

WHAT TO SAY

An all-knowing God doesn't seem a likely candidate as an amnesia victim. Peter could say of the risen Christ, "Lord, you know all things" (John 21:17). Peter's partner John could likewise affirm that God knows all things (1 John 3:20). *Omniscience* is the fancier term for God's all-knowingness.

Amazingly our all-knowing God is willing to say that he will remember our sins no more (Hebrews 10:17). Omniscience has, in effect, gotten a case of amnesia! The all-knower has become the all-forgiver-and-forgetter. We don't need to allow any confessed sins to keep us awake at night, because God has gotten amnesia about them all.

Interestingly, the *forgetter*-of-our-sins has asked *us* not to *forget*, but to remember him regularly (1 Corinthians 11:24-25).

As we remember him today at the communion table, remember that he knows all about the innermost recesses of your darkest sins. Yet he loves you. While it can be hard for us to forgive and forget the wrongs done to us by others, God knows all—and forgives all.

The communion elements are his way of saying to you today, "Though I am the only one who knows all about you, I forgive even the worst about you." Experience his forgiveness.

Chapter 8

Unveiling the Future:
Meditations From Revelation

Jesus Loves Me—This I Know

Jesus Past, Present, and Future

Somewhere Over the Rainbow

Figuring With the Figurative

The White Horse Rider

Jesus Loves Me—This I Know
Scripture: Revelation 1:5

▼ ▼ ▼ ▼ ▼ ▼ ▼ ▼ ▼ ▼ ▼ ▼ ▼ ▼ ▼ ▼ ▼

WHAT TO SAY

Victor Hugo once said that the supreme happiness of life is the conviction that we are loved.

In Revelation 1:5 we are told that Jesus "loves us." "Love" is in the present tense, a right-here-and-now, ongoing operation.

What is more profoundly simple and simply profound than the line of a children's chorus many are still taught to sing?

"Jesus loves me—this I know,

For the Bible tells me so…"

Christ died for you. Just as death separated his blood from his body, before us here are the separated bread and cup, representing his body and blood, separated in death. These elements are God's way of reminding you, that Jesus loves you right here and now.

USE THE UNUSUAL

Ask the entire congregation, including the adults, to sing "Jesus Loves Me" before or after you share communion.

Jesus Past, Present, and Future
Scripture: Revelation 1:18

▼ ▼ ▼ ▼ ▼ ▼ ▼ ▼ ▼ ▼ ▼ ▼ ▼ ▼ ▼ ▼ ▼ ▼

WHAT TO SAY

Listen to Jesus' words in Revelation 1:18: "I was dead, and behold I am alive for ever and ever." On the day of his crucifixion, it seemed that his life had been snuffed out. But three days later, he proved to be the ever-living one, having overcome death.

Our Lord is the three-tense person of the Trinity. He "was rich" in eternity past (2 Corinthians 8:9). He "was dead" after his ministry on planet Earth (Revelation 1:18). Now, by virtue of his resurrection, he's "alive for ever and ever" (Revelation 1:18). We remember him (in the present) who died (in the past) and is coming again (in the future)!

As we take communion, all these elements (past, present, and future) are with us. The bread reminds us that he died for us in the *past*. He would not take the cup again until the *future* with his disciples in the coming kingdom. And he's here with us in the *present*, for through the Holy Spirit, he's always present among us.

Today, as you "do this in remembrance of [him]" (1 Corinthians 11:24), focus on the past, present, and future character of Christ.

INTERACTIVE IDEA

Ask a participation question for the people to share with someone nearby. For example, "We often associate communion with Christ's *death*, but can you think of any ways that his *resurrection* bears upon communion?"

Somewhere Over the Rainbow
Scripture: Revelation 4:3

▼ ▼ ▼ ▼ ▼ ▼ ▼ ▼ ▼ ▼ ▼ ▼ ▼ ▼ ▼ ▼ ▼ ▼

OBJECT LESSON

Ask an artistic person in your congregation to draw a large rainbow to hang in front of your congregation. Or project a photo of a rainbow on a screen or wall.

WHAT TO SAY

Many of us grew up watching the movie *The Wizard of Oz* year after year on TV. Remember actress-singer Judy Garland's rendition of "Somewhere Over the Rainbow"?

God's patent rests on the rainbow. The rainbow is just what it sounds like—an arched bow in the sky without any arrows pointed at us (Genesis 9:13-16). God gave Noah this symbol to remind us that God is not at war with us (even though we sometimes may be at war with him).

The New Testament spells out this truth for us through another symbol—God has made peace through Christ's cross. God signs his armistice with humanity through the peace treaty of the cross of Christ (Ephesians 2:13-14).

When we see the rainbow, we can remember God's peace treaty with humanity. Interestingly, a rainbow is composed of many colors, reminding us that God communicates himself to us in many ways. One of them is communion. We *see* the rainbow; we *taste* the communion elements. They remind us that God is on peace terms with all Christians.

Today, you can *sense* God's peace-pact with you personally in a very literal way. Eat and drink and experience his peace.

Figuring With the Figurative Scripture: Revelation 5:6

▼ ▼ ▼ ▼ ▼ ▼ ▼ ▼ ▼ ▼ ▼ ▼ ▼ ▼ ▼ ▼ ▼

USE THE UNUSUAL

Ask some of the teenagers in your congregation to draw or paint or assemble a collage of overlapping pictures. You'll be talking about a Roman soldier and his helmet, a lion, a lamp, and a lamb.

BACKGROUND

When we examine certain biblical word pictures or figures of speech, it's easy to be confused by seeming inconsistencies. For example, in Ephesians 6:17, Paul describes the "helmet of salvation." Yet in 1 Thessalonians 5:8, the same word picture becomes "the hope of salvation." But biblical images don't need to be ironclad. They're flexible and fluid. God himself is so much more than our pale, earthly, one-dimensional pictures.

WHAT TO SAY

In Revelation 5:5, John called the Lord "the Lion," but in the very next verse, he proceeded to see "a Lamb" (verse 6). What's going on? These seem to be opposites. But both are true—our Lord is as majestic as a lion and as meek as a lamb.

It can get more confusing. John later describes the same *lamb* (Revelation 5:6) **as heaven's** *lamp* (Revelation 21:23).

This doesn't have to be confusing. Just as you might describe another person with multiple adjectives, such as kind, thoughtful, loving, and stubborn, it's hard to confine Christ to one figure of speech. As one song put it, he's "more than I ever dreamed of."

Do you put Christ in a box? Or have you allowed him to be multidimensional in your experience? Don't fence him in!

In communion, God supplies us with two very visual forms to communicate to us something about the reality of his love for us. From these two visual symbols, the bread and the cup, we can envision other pictures of God's expansive communication with us.

As you take part in the communion service today, meditate on the many images that Scripture uses to describe Christ, including the lion, lamb, and lamp from Revelation. Then, this week, see if you can come up with fresh analogies of how God reveals his love to you.

The White Horse Rider
Scripture: Revelation 19:11, 16

▼ ▼ ▼ ▼ ▼ ▼ ▼ ▼ ▼ ▼ ▼ ▼ ▼ ▼ ▼ ▼ ▼ ▼

BACKGROUND

Enchanting spells, handsome knights, beautiful maidens, evil witches—these are the stock in trade of fairy tales that children have loved for ages.

A long line of Prince Charmings came mounted on great steeds in fairy tales. Interestingly, the superlative theologian of Princeton, B.B. Warfield, observed that the German word for "redeem" in the New Testament is the same term used in that language's fairy tales for the prince who "breaks a spell." By redeeming us, Christ came to break Satan's evil spell.

WHAT TO SAY

Hymn writer A. Katherine Hankey said of Christ's redemption:
"More wonderful it seems
Than all the golden fancies
Of all our golden dreams."

B.J. Thomas sang,
"Storybook realities are what [Christ] gave to me,
'Cause every day you've made my dreams come true."

Christ the king is coming on a great white horse (Revelation 19:11, 16). He's the real counterpart to all the fictional wishes expressed in childhood fairy tales.

If only our prince had left us with some mystical memento, some special ring or locket to remember him by when life gets ugly, tawdry, or boring.

He has! He left us the legacy of communion. We can treat this token with special significance. It reminds us that our prince hasn't forgotten about us in our loneliness, pain, or frustration. He's coming back for us. Now, take the bread and the cup and remember him.

Scripture Index

OLD TESTAMENT

Genesis			Exodus		
2	24		12:8-9	43	
2:8	24		12:21-30	44	
2:17	22		12:31-39	31	
2:21-22	23		13:21-22	37	
3:3	22		16:4	37	
3:21	37		19:6	101	
3:23	24		19:18-19	32	
6:14	37		25	35	
9:13-16	116		25:10-22	36	
11	26		25:17	35	
11:1-9	26		25–40	34, 37	
14:18	25		26	33	
18:6-8	47		28:6-21	34	
19:3	47				
22:7	27, 28		**Leviticus**	16	38
22:8	27		16:10	37	
22:14	27		16:10, 20-22	38	
24:1-4	37		17:11	33	
28:10-17	29				
32:24, 28	25		**Numbers**	21:8-9	37
32:30-32	25				
37–47	25		**Deuteronomy**	6:4	39
37:3	30		6:4-5	39	
37:4	30		6:5	39	
37:3-10	30		18:17-20	25	
42:6	30				
43:24-34	47		**Joshua**	4:1-3	14
			4:2-3	14	

Joshua	4:6-7 14

Judges	13:2-3 40
	14–16 40
	16:17-19 40

Ruth	2:9 41
	3 41
	3:12-13 41
	4:18-22 41

| 1 Samuel | 2 . . . . 76 |

2 Samuel	4 42
	4:4 42
	9 42
	9:6-7 42
	9:3, 7 42
	9:7 13

1 Kings	4:25 29
	8:63 43
	19:12 32

| Esther | 9:18-22 . . . . . 44 |
| | 9:19 . . . . 44 |

| Job | 20:17 . . . . . . 91 |
| | 38:6-7 . . . . . . 104 |

Psalms	2:12 64
	22 46
	22:6 46
	22:12 46
	22:13 46
	22:16 . . . . . . 23, 46
	22:22 106
	23 47

Psalms	23:5 47
	27:4 48
	147:14 91

| Ecclesiastes | 3:11 . . . . 58 |

| Song of Songs | 1:12 . . . . 47 |
| | 2:4 . . . . 47 |

Isaiah	9:6 49
	38:17 50
	42:1 30
	53 54
	53:2 51
	53:3 . . . . 52, 56
	53:3-8 52
	53:5-6 53
	53:7 52
	53:7-8 . . . . . . 30, 54
	53:8 52
	53:10 41
	53:11 54
	53:12 51
	55:2 91
	63:1-3 55
	63:1-6 55
	63:2 55
	63:3 55

Ezekiel	1 56
	1:1 56
	1:4-28 56
	4:12-15 56
	5:1-4 56

Jonah	2:1-7 57
	2:2 57
	2:3 57

Micah	4:4 29
	7:19 . . . . 50, 77
Habakkuk	1:13 36
Zephaniah	3:17 106
Haggai	2:6 58
	2:7 58
	2:8 58
Zechariah	9:9 59
	9:10 59
	12:10 59
	13:6 59
	14:9 59

NEW TESTAMENT

Matthew	3:17 30
	17:5 30
	18:20 17
	22:37 37
	25:24 97
	25:37-40 19
	26:29 47
	26:36 24
	27:38 22
	27:51-52 32
Mark	4:13 11
	4:39-41 104
	10:38 57
	11:2 59
	14:22 70
	14:22-24 12
	14:25 9
	14:26 106

Mark	15:7 62
	15:9-11 62
	15:33 63
Luke	12:24 15
	15:20 64
	19:37 72
	19:39 72
	19:40 72
	22:1, 7, 15-22 . . 44
	22:19 . . . . 4, 10
	22:20 4
	24:25-26 25
	24:27 25
John	1:3 92
	1:11 30
	1:12 54
	1:14 . . . . 33, 37, 65
	1:18 49
	1:29 . . . . 27, 34
	1:47 29
	1:47-48 29
	3:14-15 37
	3:16 28
	4:42 30
	5:18 68
	6:14 . . . . 25, 104
	6:32-35 37
	8:10 75
	8:12 63
	10:3 90
	10:7 34
	13:4-5 30
	13:8 66
	14:6 . . . . 31, 34
	14:9 49
	15:1 69

John	15:1-8 24	1 Corinthians	11:20 13
	16:13 70		11:20-21. . . . 18
	16:33 49		11:20-22, 33. . 19
	17:3 54		11:24 115
	17:5 68		11:24-25. . . . 4, 111
	18:1 71		11:26 . . . . . . 9, 18,
	19:34 23		59, 98
	21:15-17 . . . 66		11:27 . . . . . . 69, 105
	21:17 . . . . . 66, 111		15:3 . . . . 53, 57
			15:3-4. 80
Acts	2:27 57		15:6 80
	2:46 18		15:45 25
	4:12 34		
	7:9 30	2 Corinthians	5:21 81
	8. 54		6:10 94
	8:30-35. . . . 30		8:9 . . . . 19, 68,
	8:32-35 . . . 54		82, 115
	10:25-26. . . 104		9:15 . . . . 36, 82
	17:28 65		11:2 23
			12:10 40
Romans	3:25 . . . . . . 34, 35,		
	36, 74	Galatians	1:4 83
	3:28 85		2:10 19
	4:4-5. 85		2:20 84
	4:6 81		5:22-23. 24
	5:15 54		
	6:7 38	Ephesians	1:7-8 94
	8:16 75		2:7 94
	8:32 28		2:8-10. 85
	8:33 75		2:10 85
	8:34 . . . . . . 34, 74		2:13-14. 116
	11:6 85		3:8 94
	11:22 76		3:16 94
	11:33 77		3:18 86
			3:20 94
1 Corinthians	1:25 40		5:25-27. . . . . 23, 37
	3:6-9. 24		6:17 117
	5:7 . . . . 37, 44		
	11:17-34. . . 18		

Philippians	1:11. 24	Hebrews	2:9 56
	1:20. 16		2:12 106
	2:5-8 87		2:14-17. 41
	2:6-8 89		4:8-10. 25
	2:7 . . . . . . 30, 87, 88		4:14. . . . . . . 34, 107, 109
	2:8 . . . . . . 26, 87		5:1 41
	2:9 89		5:1-2 76
	2:10. . . . . . 30, 90		6:19-20. . . . 108
	4:19. . . . . . 91, 94		7:1-3 25
			8:1 109
Colossians	1:17. 92		8:5 33
	2:3 . . . . . 93, 94		8:12 81
	2:8 94		9:6-9 110
	2:9 92		9:22 33
			9:25 34
1 Thessalonians	5:8 117		10:1-3. 110
			10:7 41
2 Thessalonians	1:8-10 95		10:11 110
			10:17. . . . . . 81, 111
1 Timothy	2:5 74		10:29 71
	3:16. 67		11:1 17
	6:15-16 . . . 96		11:27 17
	6:17. 97		12:1 31
			13:16 8
2 Timothy	2:8 98		
	4:8 47	1 Peter	1:8 100
			1:18-19. . . . 33
Philemon	15-16 99		1:19-20. . . . 27
	16 99		2:5, 9 101
			2:7 94
Hebrews	1–2 104		2:9 101
	1:1–3:6 . . . 104		2:23 28
	1:1-3 104		2:24 22
	1:2 92		3:20 . . . . . . 25, 37
	1:3 . . . . . . 34, 49, 105, 110	2 Peter	1:5-7 81
	1:6 104		2:13 18
	2:8 59		

1 John	1:7 . . . . 34, 46
	1:9 105
	2:2 75
	3:14 31
	3:20 111
	4:2 102
Jude	12 18
Revelation	1:5 114
	1:18 115
	2:17 90
	4:3 116
	5:5 117
	5:6 117
	5:9 58
	6:12-14 32
	8:1 32
	10:3-4 32
	12:10 75
	14:17-20 55
	19:1, 6 32
	19:9 47
	19:10 104
	19:11, 16 118
	19:16 13
	21:23 117
	22:1-2 24
	22:2 22

Story Title Index

1—Remembrance: Meditations on the Concept of Communion

Christ's Collectibles 15
"Comm" in Communion, The 8
Communion Cairns 14
From Sign to Signified 12
Golden Arches 11
Great Expectations 16
Invisible Inviter, The 17
Kuriakon 13
Once Upon a Time, Far Away 18
"Otherishness" Over Selfishness 19
Precious Memories—Let Them Linger 10
Three P's 9

2—In the Beginning: Meditations From Israel's History

Babel and Bethlehem 26
Christ Our Mercy Seat 35
Christ Our Tabernacle 33
Covering Our Crippled Condition 42
Exodus 31
Female Version of Jesus, A 44
From His Wounded Side 23
Isaac: Image of Christ 28
Jesus: Jacob's Ladder 29
Joseph, the Many-Paralleled 30
MGM Grand Rumblings 32
Old Testament Object Lessons 37
Our Kinsman Redeemer 41
Person of Persons, The 25
Protection From Perfection 36

Samsonesque Savior, The 40
Scapegoat, The 38
Stadium Ramps. 39
Tabernacle Walk-Through, A 34
Three Gardens, The. 24
Three Trees 22
What an Outdoor Barbecue. 43
Where Is the Lamb? 27

3—Poetry and Prophecy: Meditations From Psalms and the Prophets

Banqueting 47
Beauty in the Eye of the Beholder 48
Behind God's Back 50
Blessed by a Translation Error? 58
Duncan Renaldo and Our Lord 52
He for Me. 53
Multi-Titled Messiah, The 49
Old Testament Salvation 54
Splendor and Shame 56
Whale of a Time!, A 57
Where the Grapes of Wrath Are Stored. 55
Who Was That Masked Man? 51
Zechariah's Pen-Portrait 59
Zoo Story 46

4—Ministry of Jesus: Meditations From the Gospels

By George! 69
E.T. 68
I Love You. 66
Incomprehensible Incarnation 65
Lights Out! 63
Man for All Seasons, The. 62
Our Christmas Carol. 67
Silent Speakers 72
Spirit as Stagehand, The. 70
Trampled! 71
Two Kisses 64

5—**Salvation and Righteousness:** Meditations From Romans

Interceptor, The. 74
Our Double Defense 75
Softness and Severity 76
Unfathomable Depths 77

6—**The Early Church:** Meditations From the Epistles

Calvary as Auschwitz 95
Celestial Mathematics 81
Cosmic Conundrum 92
D-Day Invasion. 102
Divine Dimensions 86
Enjoyable Deity, An. 97
Gratis and Gratitude 82
Here's Richness 91
In Civvies 88
Incomparable Treasure 94
I's Have It, The 84
Old Faithful 96
Re-Circuited Relationships. 99
Sacrificial Buck Jones, The. 83
Stupendous Salvation. 85
Take Two Giant Steps 87
Thousand Sacred Sweets, A 100
Three E's, The. 80
Uncollared Priests 101
Unstuck From a Cradle or Cross! 98
What's in a Name? 90
What's "Therefore" There For? 89
X Marks the Spot 93

7—**The High Priest:** Meditations From Hebrews

All-Superior Son, The 104
Amnesiac God, The. 111
Anchored 108
Centered. 107
Herculean Task, The 105
Here It Is! 109

Singing Savior, The 106
World's Greatest Walkathon, The 110

8—Unveiling the Future: Meditations From Revelation
Figuring With the Figurative 117
Jesus Past, Present, and Future 115
Jesus Loves Me—This I Know 114
Somewhere Over the Rainbow 116
White Horse Rider, The 118